A NATION WORTH RANTING ABOUT

RICK MERCER

A NATION WORTH RANTING ABOUT

DOUBLEDAY CANADA

LIBRARY AND ARCHIVES CANADA CATALOGUING IN PUBLICATION

Mercer, Rick, 1969-
A nation worth ranting about : Rick Mercer report from across Canada / Rick Mercer.

Issued also in electronic format.
ISBN 978-0-385-67680-9

1. Canada--Politics and government--2006- --Humor.
2. Mercer, Rick, 1969- --Anecdotes. 3. Rick Mercer report (Television program). 4. Canadian wit and humor (English).
I. Title.

FC173.M464 2012 971.07'3 C2012-902378-7

Cover image: © Christopher Mason/wenn.com
Photos (except pages 6-7 and 131) © Rick Mercer Report
Printed and bound in the USA
Published in Canada by Doubleday Canada,
a division of Random House of Canada Limited

Visit Random House of Canada Limited's website:
www.randomhouse.ca

10 9 8 7 6 5 4 3 2

For Pat and Ken Mercer:

Dad for loving politics and Mom for loving saucy.

CONTENTS

ENCOUNTERS AND EXPLOITS:

A NATION WORTH RANTING ABOUT

In Whistler, B.C., with Paralympic Cross-Country Skiers Brian and Robin McKeever

Robin: "We're going to get Brian to guide you."

Brian: "The blind leading the blind."

Introduction

I have the greatest job in the country. And don't just take my word for it; I have received thousands of emails from ten-year-old boys telling me so.

With the launch of the *Rick Mercer Report,* I did not set out to work through my bucket list on national TV, but that is basically what happened. It's been a great journey.

I vividly remember, as a young boy, watching a film of an astronaut experiencing zero gravity in a NASA plane. In the film, it was made abundantly clear that the only people who would ever experience the wonder of zero gravity were the brave men and women of the space program. I pledged then and there that someday, come hell or high water, I would be a member of that program—I too would know the feeling of floating weightless high above the earth. I too would be an astronaut. When I proudly announced my ambition to the class, Miss Barnes said, "Not with your math marks, buster," and my dream fell to earth.

A greater man than I would have ignored those comments, studied hard, excelled at mathematics and science and made it into the space program, but I am not that kind of man. More than likely, I spotted something shiny and became distracted. Long story short, I never excelled at math, I went into comedy, got a TV show, and next thing you know, I was in an airplane operated by the Canadian Space Agency, experiencing zero gravity high above the nation's capital. Not a bad day at the office.

Of course, every week does not bring a bucket-list adventure. There are some adventures I would consider quite the opposite—jumping off a wharf half naked into the Atlantic Ocean in January comes to mind. But as always, despite any initial reservations I might have had about actually taking part, I don't regret it. Why? Because of the people I met along the way, every one of them great Canadians with no sense of feeling in their extremities.

Even after all these years, I am constantly amazed at the things I am allowed to do on my show. I am amazed at the quality of people I get to interview.

Take sports, for example. I have no business training with, competing against or fetching towels for the great athletes I have had the pleasure of interviewing. I am thinking in particular of Canada's amateur athletes, our Olympians and Paralympians. They are just straight-up good people. To witness the level of commitment these people have to their individual sports is truly astounding. Other than eating or sleeping, I've never come close to being as committed to anything in my entire life. Sure, the idea of being an Olympian is appealing—you represent your country on the world stage, you work to the point of physical exhaustion every day and you earn the salary of a hobo. And let's not forget that if it works out, you might get your picture taken with the Prime Minister or land a public service announcement.

I've particularly enjoyed my time with the many Paralympians who have come on the show. I am proud to say I have been beaten and humiliated in multiple sports by athletes missing every combination of limbs imaginable. And then there are the paraplegics and quadriplegics. They are the ones that leave the big bruises. Watching a game of wheelchair rugby will change forever the way you perceive anyone suffering from any form or paralysis—turns out they are happiest crashing into each other. I had no idea. Stealing a handicapped parking space is not just rude—if a member of Canada's wheelchair rugby team catches you in the act, it may be the last thing you ever do.

It's no surprise, really, that they are always fun and self-deprecating interviews. They have all had huge challenges in their lives and not only succeeded in life, but managed to become elite athletes. With everything they have had thrown at them, they are not the type of people who are about to be intimidated by a short man with a giant head and a TV camera.

I'm referring to athletes like Josh Dueck, who broke his back in a skiing accident in his teens. He woke up in a hospital to a doctor telling him he was still going to tear up the ski hill, but he was going to be doing it sitting down. I think I would have headed to the bar, but Dueck actually took him up on his challenge and within months was back on the hill. Since then, he has gone on to be a world champion sit-skier, tearing up mountains all over the world.

I can't tell you how many brilliant adventures I have had with the Canadian Forces all over Canada and overseas. I have interviewed countless soldiers and have had the opportunity to do everything from skydiving with the SkyHawks to crushing a car with a tank. In fact, I was a little put out when the news broke that Defence Minister Peter MacKay had been airlifted in a Cormorant helicopter from a fishing lodge on the Gander River. I thought, "Whoa, he's doing my act." You don't see me running out and marrying Miss World.

I'm also always amazed, when I look back at past shows, at how many vehicles I have been able to drive. In my normal life I rarely drive a car, and when I do, it's an automatic. And yet when I go to work, I get to do donuts in a hovercraft on the St. Lawrence River. I've driven stock cars, race cars, forklifts and tugboats. I have taken part in a race where three stock cars are chained together and they race against other teams of stock cars chained together. Only one car in each group of cars is allowed to have brakes. The event is called the train of death. If you take away anything from reading this book, let it be this: if anyone ever asks you to sign up for an event called "the train of death," do not do it. "Train of death" is not just a figure of speech to be ignored, like "Warning—High Voltage."

Over the years, though, the kind of adventures that I have taken part in has changed. In the old days, I was always eager to have a politician on the show. I love politics and I have always enjoyed getting a cabinet minister or a prime minister to step outside their comfort zone on TV. This has proved more difficult of late, with the advent of the electrical shock collars that the Prime Minister's Office insists that all cabinet ministers wear under their trousers. Not only does it make for a boring interview, but when some kid in the PMO pushes the button that emits the shock to the minister, it interferes with our microphones. As a result, I have basically stopped talking to cabinet ministers. Instead, I decided I would much prefer to interview a lobster fisherman or a cowboy. It was a good call; turns out Canadians like lobster fishermen and cowboys way better than politicians, and unlike politicians, they are funny and have an opinion.

So while I have almost stopped talking to politicians face to face, I continue to talk about them behind their backs. Well, some would say "talk." I would say "rant."

I do love to rant.

In fact, my name is Rick and I am a rantaholic.

A good rant is fun. A good rant is cathartic. Ranting is what keeps me sane.

The rants always come from a different place. Take the Prime Minister, for example. Sometimes when I rant about him, I am angry; other times, I am just severely annoyed—it's an important distinction.

I feel about ranting the same way the feeble-minded feel about jogging. They just don't feel complete unless they get their 10k in before breakfast. I think more Canadians should rant. It would make for a noisier but happier place. I encourage all of you to do so.

And don't feel bad if there is nobody to rant at. I rant alone all the time.

In fact, if my life had turned out differently and I wasn't on TV, I would still rant. I would just be that guy in the sales office who never shuts up.

Dear Sir or Madam,

I called your office to inquire about the availability of the two-bedroom townhouse listed on your website. The man who answered the phone refused to tell me what kind of flooring was in the property, as he was too busy yelling, "Do you realize John Baird has never had a real job?" and "How can they call themselves accountable—they run the Prime Minister's Office like it's a bloody secret society from the 1600s." Could you please tell me what kind of flooring is in the unit?

Thank you.

P.S. I checked online and I cannot find any evidence that John Baird has ever held a job in the private sector. I called the Prime Minister's Office to confirm, and they suggested I was an enemy of the state and a lover of all things Taliban.

Yours truly,
The Reverend Margaret Smith (retired)
Belleville, Ontario

Ranting is something I have always done, and I daresay I always will. Note to reader: in forty-five years, you do not want to have the bed next to me at the Performing Arts Retirement Lodge—if the soup is not up to scratch, I will be ranting about it.

Nothing makes me happier than knowing that I not only get to rant but am fortunate enough to have an audience.

It's a cliché to say that the secret to happiness is to find what it is you love and then figure out a way to make a living at it, but it is true. I've found myself saying this very same thing on stage while looking out at hundreds of eager university graduates in cap and gown. All the while, my internal monologue is saying, "Cripes, Rick, did you actually say that?"

And yet I carry on. "Canada is one of the greatest countries on earth. Do yourself a favour and get to know your country. Don't just visit its cities. Sure, stand at the top of the CN Tower someday, but make sure you stand above Canada's treeline too. I am a lucky man: every week I get to visit a new part of Canada, and every week I fall more and more in love with the country. The more you explore Canada, the more you will fall in love with it, too, and because we fight for what we love, this will make for a stronger country. This is not just a suggestion I am making; it is an obligation on your part."

It's a wonderful feeling being able to offer such sage advice to the next generation at a graduation ceremony, to look down at them and see in one room such hope, such promise, such crippling personal debt.

I know from experience I will see these young people again. I cannot tell you how many times I've been getting a coffee at Tim Hortons or having my ticket checked at Empire Cinemas, and the young man or woman in the polyester uniform will say, "Hey, you spoke at my graduation three years ago, when I got my master's degree in chemical engineering."

If time permits, I will reach out, pat them on the shoulder and ask, "Was I funny?" But I know this human contact will inevitably lead to my holding them in my arms, right there in the lobby or over the counter, rocking them gently as they sob uncontrollably over their future. "Don't worry," I say. "Tony Clement just assured Canadians again this morning that all job losses from the recession have been made up for, and it looks like you have one—congratulations!" This usually makes them feel better. Also, I carry around a business card that lists, in great length and detail, the various tax breaks and incentives that the government has introduced over the years to better insure their futures. English on one side, French on the other—both official languages.

I hope you enjoy this collection of rants and essays.

If you find that I say one thing on page 26 and the complete opposite on 72, please do not be alarmed. Simply pick the opinion that you prefer and know in your hearts that it is mine as well.

And I encourage you, the next time you see something you do not agree with, the next time you pick up a newspaper and you feel your blood boil, not to let it simmer. Rant and be merry. And rant about what you love. That's what I do.

Hence, the title of this book: *A Nation Worth Ranting About*. I believe that now more than ever.

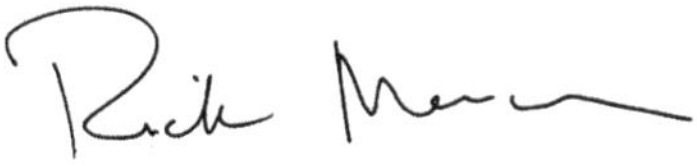

PROMISE OF BLOODSHED

September 30, 2008

So here we are, halfway through the campaign and just two nights away from the English-language leaders' debate. I know, like me, you can barely sleep. Think about it. Five individuals sitting around a table. They're going to be hot, they're going to be grumpy, they're going to be sitting next to people they don't even like. Throw in a turkey and it might as well be Thanksgiving.

I'm hoping for tears. And the drama's already there, starting with the Prime Minister.

Harper is now in majority territory, so he doesn't want to be anywhere near a debate. Don't forget, he's threatened to boycott this debate once before, if Elizabeth May was allowed in. Boy, did that backfire. Yes, kids, that man who's constantly saying he's the only one strong enough and firm enough to be a world leader is, in fact, afraid of the girl. And not only does he have to deal with the girl, Jack Layton and a desperate separatist, but for the first time since the start of this campaign, he is going to have to come face to face with Stéphane Dion.

On the surface, that does not seem like a big deal.

But remember back to high school, folks. Remember when the nerdy kid finally had enough of being slapped around by the bully and he said, "Okay, I'll meet you at the lockers." Everyone showed up for that fight.

Because this is not a normal political rivalry. This is personal. Never mind that the Tories have spent millions of dollars calling Dion a pathetic loser; lately, they've been going after his wife. And don't forget: on day one of this campaign, Harper wouldn't even admit that Dion had a real family. People with adopted children are very touchy about that sort of thing. Personally, I wouldn't be surprised if Dion snaps and takes a smack at him.

So, never mind democracy; tune in for the promise of bloodshed, and maybe if we're lucky, a knockout punch. And remember: traditionally, in Canada, the real campaign begins on debate night. So from here on in, anything is possible. And for the first time in a long time, thankfully, nobody can say, "May the best man win."

Sitting in as Speaker at the annual Queen's University Model Parliament, Ottawa.

Rick: "Before we get going, I know we're about to debate this bill, but I would like to have each and every one of you practise a few things. The first thing you have to be able to do is nod, no matter what your leader says."

THEY DON'T CARE ABOUT STUDENTS

October 7, 2008

So here it is, the final stretch before the big vote, and all the political parties are busy courting every special-interest group in the country, no matter how small. If you've got one leg, two kids, you work on a farm, then the parties, they have a pitch for you. Unless, of course, you happen to be a student, in which case you're completely off the radar. There hasn't been a peep from any of the leaders about education. It wasn't even mentioned in the debate.

Now, I'm not saying that any politician would ever come out and say they don't care about the student vote. When they're pushed, they can all talk about educational reform and crushing debt until the cows come home, but at the ten-minute mark they all do the same thing. They stop, they lean in like they're telling you some sort of secret and they say, "You know, it's a real shame. But students in this country, they just don't vote." Which, believe me, is code for "We don't care about students. We never have and we never will."

Now, this is a perfect example of where young people can learn from their elders. And by elders,

I mean the elderly. As in senior citizens. Because those folks, they vote. Which is why the old-age home is the natural habitat for any campaigning politician. No exaggeration: of the thirty days since this campaign began, John Baird has spent twenty-six of them in an old-age home. Okay, *slight* exaggeration.

I'm not suggesting that students themselves aren't important to politicians. Oh, you are. After all, you're the ones that deliver the lawn signs. But past that, you could be on fire for all they care. So my advice to university students is: Never mind your civic responsibility. Seeing as you're such a low priority in this country, you should show up and vote out of spite, if for no other reason.

There are a million students in this country. If you actually show up and vote, elections will never be the same again. Education will never be left off the agenda. And all you students out there who are living away from home for the first time? Ignore all those Elections Canada ads that make it seem like you need quantum physics to vote. In this country, you do not need to be registered in advance to vote. Men died on the beaches so you could vote. All you need to do is to show up with some official-looking mail with your address on it, your student card and your ID. Don't take no for an answer, and democracy is yours.

And not your fake ID, either. Your real one.

Saying it loud and clear at the University of Guelph.

THE CANADIAN PRESS/Sean Kilpatrick

VOTE MOB? WHAT'S A VOTE MOB? I HAD NO IDEA THIS HAD SOMETHING TO DO WITH ME.

THE FIRST TIME I heard the expression "vote mob" was from a reporter for the Canadian Press. I have few skills, but one of them is that I can blather on at great length on many subjects. That said, as a rule, I have learned to avoid blathering away on subjects I know absolutely nothing about and stick to what I know: politics, and where to get the food in any Canadian town with a population of over six hundred. I've learned that if you don't know the answer, there is no shame in saying, "Honestly? I have no idea what the Toronto Maple Leafs should do heading into the draft deadline, although I'm sure Ron James does, or everyone else in the city, for that matter."

So when a journalist called and asked me about my reaction to the "vote mob," I was happy to plead ignorance. I honestly didn't know what the reporter was talking about. The reporter thought I was pulling a fast one. "How can you say you don't know about the vote mob?" she said. "It was your idea."

Talking to a member of the media on the record and having them suggest you might have something to do with a mob you've never heard of is not an ideal situation. Instantly, I took diplomatic leave of the conversation. "I'm sorry—the flight attendant is telling me I have to turn my phone off. I'll call back when I land in Iqaluit."

When you are someone who appears quite often on television, you sometimes get the blame or credit for things you have had nothing to do with. It goes with the territory. Sometimes people confuse people on TV with other people on TV for no other reason than they are both on TV. I once got an email that said, "Dear Mr. Mercer, I was watching you yesterday at 3:00 on Channel 603, and what you said to that little boy who lost his dog in Hurricane Katrina was truly wonderful. I'm sure he will love the puppy you sent him." I mentioned it to my sister, and she said, "Oh, I watched that. It was Oprah."

So yes, because I am on TV, I have been confused with an African-American woman in her late fifties. I'm not complaining; there are worse people to be confused with. Everyone loves Oprah, and frankly it's not nearly as upsetting as being confused with Rex Murphy. That hurts.

Within seconds of hanging up from the reporter, I Googled "vote mob," and all was revealed.

"Vote Mob—University of Guelph" was trending on YouTube. It was already a day old, which made me feel a little better; if an actual mob had done anything mobbish, like burn down a faculty building, I assume I would have heard about it by now. But still, I had no idea what this had to do with me.

When I hit play, the first thing that came up in big, bold letters was the statement "Rick Mercer encouraged young people to vote—Rick, this one is for you." And that is how I saw my first vote mob.

I have to tell you, a vote mob is a beautiful sight. I feel about vote mobs the way some people feel about sunsets, or the way Justin Trudeau feels about mirrors. I can stare at them all day. There they were, hundreds of kids at the University of Guelph, saying loud and clear that in the coming election, they would be voting. They were dancing and singing and waving Canadian flags. There was nothing anti-government in the message. There was nothing partisan in the message. The message was simple: we love Canada and we are voting. If you look at the voter turnout among young people in this country, this is a radical message.

It turns out the vote mob was the brainchild of two brilliant young women from Guelph, Gracen Johnson and Yvonne Su. These are the kind of young people that make you believe everything will be all right with the world. They are whip smart, involved, passionate, articulate and, when it comes to the issue of young people voting, very pissed off.

Well, at least we had the latter in common.

A few months previous, I was flying to Ottawa and bumped into a guy I've known semi-professionally for many years. He was, for as long as I'd known him, a political party activist and worker.

He was heading to Ottawa for a meeting with the central campaign office. This is the kind of meeting that young politicos live for. Being summoned to Ottawa to meet with a campaign director meant he was going to the big time. His years of campaigning all over the country were about to pay off. A federal election was going to be called sooner rather than later, and for a politico of his stripe there was only one place to be: the central campaign headquarters, a spot in the war room. This was like being told to suit up for the playoffs.

Weeks later, I bumped into our young hero back in Toronto. I asked how that Ottawa meeting went and he told me, "Not well." In fact, he had just accepted a job in New York and was leaving in a few days. He would be sitting out the election. "They screwed me," he said. "They had nothing to offer. In fact, they had less than nothing."

He didn't need very much prompting to tell me what happened.

"They offered me youth outreach," he informed me. The way he said it—"*They offered me youth outreach*"—reminded me of an actor saying "I didn't get the part" after a third callback for the lead role that eventually went to someone who was sleeping with the producer.

Now, this entire exchange confused me. From where I was standing, being in charge of youth outreach seemed to be a good gig. And this guy, having come up through campus politics, was obviously well qualified. When I said, "Youth outreach? Come on, that's good," he looked at me like I was perhaps the stupidest person in his time zone. How could I have gotten this far in life and understand so little?

And once again, for the umpteenth time, I got a lesson in how politics really works from the people who actually practise the art, as opposed to people like me who blather about it.

"Youth outreach isn't real," he said. "If you're in charge of youth outreach, you are lucky to get a BlackBerry and a desk, let alone a staff or an organization. In fact, the job of youth outreach is first and foremost to fill a slot so the party can say, 'We have someone in charge of youth outreach,' on the off chance someone from the media asks the question, which they won't."

Apparently, youth outreach is where ambitious young party workers go to die. He explained to me, in no uncertain terms, that young people don't vote, they won't be part of any national discussion during the election, and nobody in the central campaign has any interest in that happening. The dude making coffee at election headquarters will be more influential than whatever poor sucker ends up running youth outreach.

Oh. My bad.

Now, don't get me wrong—I know very well that all political parties rely heavily on youth, but they rely on actual young people who volunteer for the party. These bodies do the heavy lifting, they make phone calls, they deliver lawn signs and, most importantly, they show up and bang thunder sticks together like demented monkeys for a local candidate who can barely string a sentence together. Political parties love the young in the same way that major clothing manufacturers love the Chinese—because they represent free labour. Past that, they can go pound sand.

Political parties know, or they have decided, that any energy spent on encouraging young people to vote is a waste of time and resources. They believe that young people won't vote, and sadly, the numbers back them up.

And so I ranted. I figured, "Okay, young people don't vote—fine, they have their reasons." But nobody, no matter how complacent they are, likes to be taken advantage of, and that is exactly what every modern political party in Canada was doing with young people.

So I ranted.

And according to YouTube, the kids at the University of Guelph were either listening, or they were the exception to the rule. They weren't just voting, they were organizing.

And so I watched my first vote mob on YouTube, and it turns out I wasn't the only one. The number of views continued to ramp up; suddenly, the video was being shared on Facebook pages across the country and Twitter was on fire with the hash tag #votemob.

And then a wonderful thing happened: it began to spread.

At the University of Guelph, as at most universities across the country, it was exam time. Gracen Johnson and Yvonne Su holed up in one of their bedrooms and studied for their finals, planned Guelph's second vote mob and Skyped with students across Canada who were reaching out to them for advice.

The University of Victoria, then McMaster and Memorial University in Newfoundland and Labrador all started posting vote mobs. Every province and territory was represented. Over forty-five individual vote mobs took place within days.

Of course, the mainstream media began to pay attention, and that begat more vote mobs. Suddenly, parties were being asked what they were doing to reach out to young voters and encourage young people to vote.

Their answers were uniformly pathetic. Politicians were the last to figure out what was happening, and many of them were confused. John Baird said he found the entire thing disconcerting.

Michael Taube, Stephen Harper's former speechwriter, was apoplectic that students across the country were assembling and threatening to actually vote. In a special column for the *Ottawa Citizen,* he wrote: "A few weeks ago, there was no such thing as a 'vote mob.' But an idea hiding in a deep, dark corridor of comedian Rick Mercer's brain has, quite by accident, unleashed this holy terror onto unsuspecting Canadians.

"Do you really think," he wrote, admonishing the kids in the videos, "that any of the major leaders honestly cares that some 18-25-year-olds who wouldn't ordinarily vote have suddenly been convinced by a comedian's rant on TV?"

Taube's tongue was not in his cheek—but it's clear where his head was as he ended his column with a plea to maintain the status quo: "If vote mobs are ever considered to be a viable method of increasing political participation, I would much rather keep the numbers as low as they are."

Yes, a former speechwriter for Stephen Harper was telling the world that politics in Canada would be better served if young people simply stayed home.

As voting day got closer, another problem presented

itself to the organizers of the Guelph mobs. Students who wanted to vote were leaving university and heading back to their home ridings because the school year was over. Thousands of students all over the country who wanted to vote were in flux, stuck between the riding they lived in to attend school and the ridings their parents lived in. Many students were leaving to go to summer jobs in areas where they weren't qualified to vote. The simple solution, the organizers believed, consisted of advance ballots on campus. The argument being, there are advance polls in senior citizens' homes and neighbourhoods all over Canada, so why not on campus?

Elections Canada set one up, and their workers were nearly overwhelmed by the number of students that actually showed up. Students lined up by the hundreds.

When news of the huge turnout made it to the various political campaigns—or one in particular—panic hit. The communications director for the Conservative Party candidate, a young man by the name of Michael Sona, ran up and down the line, declaring loudly that the Elections Canada polling station was illegal. He then attempted, according to numerous eyewitnesses, to do something unheard of in Canada: take the ballot box.

It has been suggested that while officials at Elections Canada certainly reminded Sona that interfering with a person's right to vote was a serious offence in Canada, some students in line used more colourful language to convince him that he wouldn't be going anywhere with the ballot box. Sona left and the voting continued.

For Sona, it was a good day at the office. Not only did his willingness to disrupt a polling station land him on the front pages of newspapers all across the country, it caught the attention of the people running the Conservative campaign. That boy has moxie! He is their kind of people. After the election, he would travel to Ottawa, where he would go to work as a political staffer for the parliamentary secretary to the Minister of National Defence. He was headed for the big time. Sadly, his career came to an end when he resigned over his alleged involvement in the robocall/voter-suppression scandal that began in, you guessed it, Guelph.

I attended only one vote mob during the election. It turned out to be the nation's largest, and it took place in London, Ontario. Thousands of people, not just university students, showed up to wave flags, announce they were voting and encourage others to follow suit. It was the most fun I've ever had. The video is one of my favourite YouTube videos to this day.

I think the vote mobs were the most exciting thing that happened during that election. I loved every single one of them that I watched online. And I was never so proud as when writers like Michael Taube blamed me for the entire thing. It felt good knowing someone that close to the Prime Minister was that pissed off at me.

But the vote mobs started in Guelph with Gracen Johnson and Yvonne Su. Many months later, I was looking at the timeline of the entire adventure, and I realized my rant about young people voting aired just two days before that first vote mob. I called Gracen and suggested that while I knew she and Yvonne were geniuses, two days seemed a little tight. She would only say that she appreciated the rant.

Sometimes a guy rants at the right time. And sometimes if you are on TV, you get the credit or the blame for something you had nothing to do with. I am proud to accept both in this instance.

But more than anything, I look forward to voting for Gracen and Yvonne someday, and if I'm not eligible I'll show up and knock on some doors.

LET'S SEE WHAT THEY'RE UP TO

October 14, 2008

At the risk of sounding like an out-of-touch elite weirdo, I confess I have on occasion walked into a theatre, bought a ticket, sat down and watched a play. And my favourite moment is when the lights go dark and the audience goes quiet. Because at that moment, anything is possible.

I feel the same way about election night. Tonight, the House of Commons is an empty stage. And I can't help but think that maybe, just maybe, this time, this Parliament will get it right, and be brilliant. Now, I've never seen that happen in my lifetime. The difference being, of course, that in the theatre, the people on stage are actually trying, and there's nowhere to hide. Whereas in the House of Commons, nobody—other than the few people sitting in the gallery—can see what the MPs are doing.

And believe me, they're out of control. I get embarrassed watching Question Period live, and I've been naked on national television. Imagine going in to your office or your workplace tomorrow, and the minute you see anyone you don't like, you just start yelling and screaming like a lunatic. You'd be fired.

And there's a reason. Because when people act like that, nothing gets done at work. It's not acceptable in any Canadian workplace. Why is it acceptable on Parliament Hill?

There is a solution: cameras. Cameras in the House of Commons. Not just on the people who are supposed to be talking, but on everyone else. The MPs, of course, would say, "Cameras? That's terrible. You're treating us like criminals or children." And yes, we would be. And hell, every time I go into the subway I'm on a camera. If Parliament were fitted with them too, whenever MPs decided to disrupt Parliament intentionally by acting like idiots, the entire country could see them doing it. And then maybe, just maybe, the bad acting would disappear and we'd finally get a show that makes us proud.

With the women of the Montreal Roller Derby League.

Rick: "I didn't mean to touch that many bums, but it was just—it's a lot of bums in there."

Player: "It's one of the key benefits of the sport."

HOW TO CHOOSE A LOSER

October 21, 2008

The week or so after a federal election is a period of reflection for political parties. As we speak, the Conservatives might be saying, "Wow, I guess we just didn't give enough to Quebec—maybe we should give them more." And the NDP might be saying, "Yes! We did it. We came in last. For the sixteenth time in a row. Well done, people." And for the Liberals? How do I put this nicely? Let's just say it's pretty clear at this point that nobody will ever make a movie of the week about Stéphane Dion. Not even a fully funded CBC.

In politics, of course, people lose all the time. But it always comes as a huge shock to the Liberals, because they like to believe they are *the natural governing party of Canada*. That's a phrase that harkens back to 1896—and nothing much in the party has changed since.

Look at the way the Liberals choose a leader. Members of the party don't actually get to vote for the leader—oh no, no, no, that would be madness. Instead, they choose a delegate. And when they choose their delegate, they hoist them up on their shoulders and they march them down to the train station and then send them off to Montreal somewhere. And then, three days later, some guy named Gerard Kennedy makes a backroom deal and then, suddenly, the guy in third place who can't communicate becomes the leader. Then there's an election. Then they lose.

Here's an idea. From now on, how about members of the party actually get to vote for the leader? And instead of these old fashioned multimillion-dollar conventions, do it on the Internet. Hell, you can do your banking on it, you can buy a kidney on it—surely to God you can figure out a way to vote for the leader of a political party on it.

The point is, if the Liberal Party ever wants to be relevant ever again, it's time for them to rebuild that party from the ground up. Which is a nice way of saying it's time to break out the Bic lighter and the gasoline. And the beauty of it is, the time is now—because no matter what changes they make, they can't screw it up any more than it is already.

WHO'S IT GONNA BE?

October 28, 2008

In these uncertain economic times, it's nice to know that some things do not change. The leaves turn. The snow falls. And then there's a Liberal leadership convention.

The smart money says this will be an epic battle between Michael Ignatieff and Bob Rae. Some sort of unavoidable, preordained fight to the death that was first prophesied in ancient scripture. And if the entire party is destroyed in the process, then so be it. Which is why a lot of Liberals are once again looking for that long-shot candidate who can sneak up the middle and stop them all from being annihilated. Justin Trudeau. Will he run? I have no idea. But I know this: mere mortals such as you or me cannot believe the pressure he is under to run. A lot of Liberals out there, they see Justin Trudeau and go mushy in the head. And when you tell them that he has no experience in politics, they say it doesn't matter, he grew up around it.

Now, this I understand. My father worked for the Department of Fisheries and Oceans for twenty years, and I cannot tell you how many times complete strangers have suggested that I should be put in charge of turbot fish quotas.

And then there's Gerard Kennedy. *Hi, remember me? I'm the guy who gave you Dion.* Now for the Liberals to go with Kennedy at this point . . . that's a bit like necking with the guy at the office Christmas party that gave you the cold sore—twice. But hey, stranger things have happened. And then, of course, there's the dream of the white knight. Will a Frank McKenna just show up out of the blue and save the party? Now, this is interesting, because usually, in most countries, when they're talking about dream candidates, they throw around adjectives like *brilliant, charismatic, dynamic.* Whereas in Canada, only one adjective counts: bilingual. Yeah, Barack Obama wouldn't cut it up here.

But to any Liberals out there who can't make up their minds, I say, don't worry—at the rate your party is going, with three leadership conventions in five years, eventually, everyone's going to get a turn.

Skating with Tie Domi on Battle of the Blades, *at Maple Leaf Gardens, Toronto.*

Guest judge Don Cherry (wiping away a tear): "Oh, that was beautiful. Mercer and Domi—poetry on ice."

FATTER AND DUMBER

November 4, 2008

Stephen Harper has at last ended speculation and named a new cabinet. And my goodness, the tough decisions he had to make. I mean, there he was, elected in the middle of an unprecedented global economic meltdown, with the promise that he would never increase spending, with the promise that he would never bring us into deficit, and what's the very first thing he does? Increase his cabinet by six members. Stephen Harper now has thirty-eight cabinet ministers. In 1993, Jean Chrétien had twenty-three.

This is why Canadians hate politicians. In the light of what is going on in the world right now, there is not a Canadian out there who runs a business, a charity or a household who didn't sit down this month and say, "You know what? I've got to figure out how to cut costs." And they did—except for Stephen Harper, who said, "Six new Tories get a $75,000-a-year raise, plus limos."

Stephen, here's an idea: if you really want to make room in cabinet for new people, why don't you just fire all the old cabinet ministers who were lousy at their jobs? There's plenty of them.

Remember, folks, this is the government whose Minister of Health was unavailable for comment for five weeks when Canadians started dropping dead from eating sandwiches. But don't worry. He got a big promotion. So who got demoted? I love this. Jim Prentice.

Why Jim Prentice? Because Jim is the guy that all the Tories secretly talk about as replacing Stephen Harper someday. Because everyone knows that Jim is the smartest guy in caucus, and plus, people like him.

So what did Stephen Harper give to him? Minister of the Environment. Which, with this crowd, in this government, is the same as being Minister of Your Career Is Now Dead. So here we are, folks. We elected a man who promised that he would put a firm hand on the tiller. And he certainly has. Except the ship just got fatter and dumber.

CLASH OF THE TITANS

November 18, 2008

So, the Liberal leadership race is well underway and looks like it'll be a clash of the titans. Michael Ignatieff vs. Bob Rae—and the wild card being that young fellow Dominic Leblanc.

Now, this is a leaner, meaner race than in 2006, and both front-runners are in a far better position than they were then. In 2006, the Tories ran a vicious stealth campaign against Bob Rae, accusing him of being in power during a recession. Well, the Tories now have their own recession and their own deficits to deal with.

Back then, they accused Ignatieff of being an outsider. This time around, the man has a Canadian driver's licence. And he knows the difference between the Calgary Stampede and Blue Rodeo. That's gotta help.

But the big news for the cash-strapped Liberal Party is that this time around, both Bob Rae and Michael Ignatieff are in their sixties. Which means if they campaign by train, they're now eligible for the VIA Rail seniors' discount. Dominic Leblanc won't be able to do that for another twenty years. Which reminds me: who the hell is Dominic Leblanc, anyway? All I really know about the guy is that he's got more experience in the House of Commons than Bob Rae and Michael Ignatieff combined, and the Tories want him to win because he has a French last name and a horrible secret.

The secret? He studied law at Harvard—which, according to the Conservatives, is a huge character flaw. Yes, apparently we're now a nation that lies awake at night, terrified that our children might want to go to a really good university.

Oh—and the other thing about Dominic Leblanc is that, like Bob Rae and Michael Ignatieff, he's a very good speaker in not one, but two official languages. So no matter who wins, the Tories are in for a few sleepless nights as well.

SNOW TIRES

November 25, 2008

I'm one of those Canadians who like winter. Sure, I think it lasts too long, but still I like to see it coming. So when we had the first snowfall here in Toronto, I went for a walk. And with the snowflakes gently falling against the streetlights, I wandered around the city for about half an hour and I enjoyed the sights and sounds of thirteen fender-benders in nine languages.

Yes, it was a winter wonderland, interrupted only when some guy in an Audi locked up his brakes and slid headfirst into a telephone pole about three feet from my legs.

Then he jumped out and said, "Don't move! I might need a witness." And I'm thinking, What's he need a witness for? What's he gonna do, say it wasn't his fault, that the pole jumped in front of his car? And then, when I asked him later if he had snow tires on, he looked at me like I was an idiot and said, "I don't need snow tires—I've got all-season radials."

This is what I want to know. How can a guy be smart enough to have a job that lets him drive a $59,000 car and be stupid enough to say he doesn't need snow tires when he's standing next to his Audi that's wrapped around a pole? This is Canada. There's no such thing as all-season tires, just like there's no such thing as all-season footwear. There is in southern California. They're called flip-flops. You wear them in all seasons up here, you'll end up with no feet.

The first sign of flurries in Toronto, the entire place becomes a bumper-car track. No exaggeration—the provincial police said there were nine hundred fender-benders in Toronto in the first five centimetres of snow. This is a crisis, Ontario. There's no shame in being a have-not province; being a can't-drive province—that's just embarrassing.

Driving in the snow is like sex. If you want to avoid accidents, abstinence is the best policy. But if you're going to take a spin, use protection.

BAD MAN IN A CRISIS

December 2, 2008

We might as well get it over with and admit it: Stephen Harper is a genius.

Here we are in the midst of a global economic crisis. Nations all over the world are desperately trying to help their citizens—who are terrified. We have seen unheard-of acts of co-operation among political rivals all over the industrialized world.

Not in Canada. Not with Stephen Harper. Not on his watch. No, my friends, Stephen Harper has one goal and one goal only, and it has nothing to do with governing: How could he use this crisis to destroy the Opposition? And wouldn't you know it, he almost did it.

Harper decided Canada didn't need any kind of economic stimulus. Oh no, all we needed to do was cancel the subsidies to political parties—a move that would have saved about $26 million. Or about the same amount of money that Harper now spends every year on bodyguards when he travels to danger zones like Thunder Bay or Nunavut.

But of course, the real upside for Harper in all of this was that it would have destroyed or crippled the

Opposition. It gives me great faith, knowing that as our economy collapses, Harper is on the job, coming up with new and innovative ways to interfere with the Green Party's office budget and bankrupt the Liberals. And who knows, maybe then the world will be a better place.

Maybe he has a point. Maybe that's why Canada won't give this guy a majority. It's not because he's a mean little man obsessed with revenge, it's because we just have too many choices. We walk into the voting booth, we get confused. It's kind of like that first trip to Baskin Robbins. Maybe we'd all be better off if Conservative was the only flavour on the menu.

Well, we almost found out. Because if Harper had gotten away with this, democracy in this country would have changed forever. And not a single citizen would have voted on the matter.

Guest starring on the Weather Network in Oakville, Ontario.

Rick: "And then we have St. John's, Newfoundland, of course . . . and it's freezing and Dad's complaining about the weather and I've never heard him complain before, so that can't be good. Plus, his leg hurts."

FORGIVE THEM, CANADA

The Globe and Mail, *December 6, 2008*

Not long after Stephen Harper took office as Canada's twenty-second prime minister, a polar bear was born at the Berlin Zoo. Known as Knut, the cub was rejected by his mother, and so was nursed by human beings. Now, two years later, animal psychologists say that he has become so addicted to human laughter and applause that the instant those things disappear, he becomes desolate and cries for attention. This has led to irrational behaviour never before seen in a polar bear. Experts fear that, without constant applause, Knut could lose the will to live.

Enter Stephen Harper.

During the past week, while the nation wondered if the government would fall, junior Conservative staffers were ordered to be outside 24 Sussex Drive by six-fifteen in the morning. Their job was to stand there in the dark, with the temperature well below zero, and wait for the PM to appear. Their instructions were to applaud, wave and sing "O Canada" loudly as the motorcade pulled out of the gates and drove Stephen Harper to work.

Harper, by all accounts, actually believed that the young people were there of their own accord and represented a groundswell of love and support for his actions. Staffers in the Prime Minister's Office know that he is easier to handle when being applauded and not questioned. This way, nobody has to suffer at the hands of the inconsolable bear.

Enter Stéphane Dion.

Dion is a humiliated and beaten man. Nothing prepared him for the thrashing he took in the last election, and the subsequent rejection by his own party just made matters worse. For him, the applause and cheering stopped a long time ago. Given the chance to exact revenge, he seized it.

And so, is it any surprise that these damaged, needy men are the architects of a parliamentary crisis the likes of which we have never seen? With leaders like this, we shouldn't be blamed for asking, "Why bother?"

If this Parliament were a dog, it would be brought out behind the shed and shot. Rabid dogs aren't prorogued, reformed or trusted.

At first, this little crisis in Ottawa was good, old-fashioned fun—blood sport for political junkies that made for great entertainment.

It began, of course, with the government's economic statement, a colossal misstep for Stephen Harper. The nastiness and partisanship caught everyone off guard.

Sane cabinet ministers had to grin and bear it as the leader revealed a strategy that not only highlighted the very worst elements of his personality, but reinforced the nagging cliché that this Conservative Party cares more about inflicting pain on those they dislike than offering support for anyone in need.

Harper, the self-professed master strategist, figured this was one game of hardball he could not lose, but then a funny thing happened on the way to the vote in the House of Commons.

Dion may lack the basic skills needed by all political leaders, but he has a grasp of basic math, something the PM, an economist, seems to have lost. Dion crunched the numbers and realized that not only could the government fall, he could even become prime minister. Revenge like that comes once in five lifetimes.

In theory, a coalition could work. If aliens from outer space were running roughshod over the country, perhaps a Liberal, a socialist and a separatist could put their differences aside and work together to defeat the alien overlords. A global economic crisis, however, is probably not enough for these three wildly divergent visions of Canada to gel.

But whether the coalition can or will survive is irrelevant; what matters is that it can oust the PM.

Stephen Harper loves being the Prime Minister of

Canada. Since he came to power, the motorcades have got longer, the office more presidential, the trappings more grand. The idea that he could suddenly find himself standing in line at the airport with regular Canadians, photo ID at the ready, attempting to board a Jazz flight to Moncton so he can explain to party faithful why he now travels in a Jiffy Taxi gnaws at his very being.

Knut the polar bear could not survive such a humiliation, and neither could Harper. So he slapped his finance minister and tore up the economic update; he blinked and backtracked—behaviour not before seen in this political animal.

And this is where it should have ended: a substantial and unexpected victory for a lame-duck Liberal leader and a humiliating lesson to the Prime Minister. A nice little reminder to all involved that nobody was granted a majority in this Parliament, and we expect everyone to get along.

Tragically, Dion wasn't strong enough to put on the brakes. Or more likely, he was unwilling.

Enter the Governor General of Canada.

Try explaining this one to those alien overlords: thirty-five million people, in one of the greatest democracies on earth, stare at their television sets, waiting to see whether an unelected former TV broadcaster will choose to shut down our government for over a month or let it live just long enough to be killed by the Opposition.

The drama that played out this week was many things: unimaginable, embarrassing, and yes, it made our parliamentary system look like a laughingstock. However, this situation was not, as Harper insisted, undemocratic, illegal or un-Canadian.

The facts are clear. He has a minority in the Commons—something he has never accepted. So he loves daring the Opposition to defeat him, and prides himself on shaming them at every opportunity.

But them's the rules, and he knows it. And yet, when faced with actually losing a confidence vote, he chooses to launch a full-fledged attack on the very institution he is sworn to protect. He took to the airwaves, saying that having him lose a vote would amount to a *coup d'état*. He knows this isn't true, but he said it anyway. Then his ministers fanned out and told everyone who would listen that an election was being stolen. They shouted from the rooftops that, as a nation, we elected Stephen Harper to lead us, that the 308 members of Parliament actually had no say in the matter.

Harper zeroed in on Quebec. The master strategist who has wooed that province for the past two years turned anything and anyone with a French name into a whipping boy. Memo to Quebec: call Danny

Williams. A world of hurt is coming your way. And our prime minister suggested that, in a constitutional crisis, the Governor General must not listen to constitutional advisers, but to him and him alone. The Prime Minister's Office organized a protest at the Governor General's residence. Staffers all over Ottawa were given the day off to stand there waving signs reading "The Bloc Sucks" and "Stop the Coup." Surely the Queen was not amused.

Back on Parliament Hill, Minister of Bluster John Baird proudly announced that Conservatives would go over the head of Parliament and of the Governor General. He planted the seed for what sounds like the Republic of Canada, in which Harper and not the monarch is the head of state. One assumes that a Harper republic will differ from others in the world, as he ostensibly will have majority powers without having that old-fashioned 50-percent support in either the country or the Commons.

All this made for a perfect storm. Our system works on the assumption that, regardless of whether we have a minority government, we will always be guaranteed of having a clear and decisive majority of rational men and women who will, in times of crisis, put nation over personal or party interests. It operates on the assumption that our leaders will put country before party.

Seems we are out of luck on that front—our bad.

The crisis has not ended, but simply has been postponed. In the new year, Stephen Harper will return with the biggest-spending budget in Canadian history. People who voted Conservative will be outraged, but their cries will be drowned out by the applause of the paid staffers again lining the sidewalk outside 24 Sussex. Knut the polar bear will bask in the adoration.

And, yes, the coalition may survive long enough to defeat them anyway—revenge being a dish best served at the first possible opportunity.

Meanwhile, this great democracy of ours has ceased to function. We have no government because they just can't get along. It is a mess that defies comprehension but has one simple solution. We need one more strange-bedfellows event: a historic press conference at which Stephen Harper and Stéphane Dion apologize to their country and then to their parties. And then they resign—no questions, please.

Because they deserve one another—and Canada deserves better.

With Jann Arden on the CN Tower Edgewalk.

Jann: "I can't do it! I seriously can't!"

Rick: "This will make you calm. We're walking down the street. Jann—

I heard you wrote a book. What's the name of your book?"

Jann: "You id-"

Rick: "What's the name of your book?"

Jann: "*Falling Backwards*!"

ASLEEP AT THE WHEEL

January 13, 2009

A month before Christmas, it looked like the Harper government was going to collapse and be replaced with a coalition. A very interesting scenario, and for a lot of people, not a very nice one. But like it or not, our system is designed that way.

But the truly astounding thing was, in the middle of the whole fiasco, the Dominion Institute did a poll and they found out that a majority of Canadians had no idea what was going on, and in fact lacked a basic understanding of our parliamentary system. This is a crisis. And what did our own government do? They went out of their way to make it worse.

They had ministers go on TV and say this was a *coup d'état,* that coalitions were illegal and undemocratic. John Baird said his government had the right to ignore the will of Parliament altogether and go over the head of the Governor General.

None of which is true. How can a country function when half the population doesn't know what the hell is going on and their own government actually likes it that way? Being a good citizen is like driving a car. We all have to know the basic rules of the road.

We don't have to *like* the rules—we can even get together and change the rules. But we all have to know how to proceed when dealing with a four-way stop or a blinking red.

And it doesn't matter if John Baird is in the back seat saying, "No, no, no, go straight on through, don't stop." We know we have to stop, look both ways, and then floor it.

Canada is no different. We are a parliamentary democracy. And that system has served us well for 141 years. But clearly, we've fallen asleep at the wheel. And if we want to protect this democracy, we all have an obligation to wake up and get informed. Because our members of Parliament can't be trusted with it anymore.

OBAMA'S EXAMPLE

January 20, 2009

It's inauguration day in America, and like everyone else, I can't help but get caught up in the moment. As a Canadian, I did not believe in my lifetime I would see a man like Barack Obama become president of the United States. And not because he's black, but because he ran a positive campaign and actually got elected. And if recent history has taught us anything, it's that that could never work up here.

When it comes to politics, we haven't seen anything remotely positive in a very long time. Think about it. In the last American election, the defining themes were "change is possible" and "hope." And they had the highest voter turnout in forty years. In our last election, the defining themes were "stay the course" and "destroy the enemy." And we had the lowest voter turnout in our entire history.

Clearly, we are on two different tracks. Which is fine—we are a sovereign nation, we are unique on the world stage. For example, we're now the last nation on earth that wants Guantanamo Bay prison to stay open, and it's not even our prison.

Yes, it's a brave new world, and we're old school.

Now, that doesn't mean we shouldn't celebrate the new president. Everyone loves this guy. Cripes, when Obama announced that his first foreign visit was going to be to Canada, Stephen Harper looked so excited I thought his head was going to pop off.

I don't blame him. I'd like to get my picture taken with Obama, too. And clearly, the fact that he's visiting Canada is very exciting, because, as of today, he is the forty-fourth president of the United States—and eight hours in, he's doing a bang-up job.

He got that job by doing something that no Canadian political leader has done in a very long time. He appealed to the very best in his fellow citizens and gave them something to believe in. So when the visit finally happens, let's hope some of that rubs off.

SPENDING IN SECRET

January 27, 2009

Budget day in Canada is one of the few times of the year when Canadians pay attention to how the government is spending our money. And believe me, governments hate that. They would much prefer to operate in total secrecy. It's in their nature.

But luckily, we have the Freedom of Information Act. Which says if you or I or a journalist has a legitimate question about how our government is spending the money, they have to answer it. And just to make sure they do, we have an information commissioner, Robert Marleau, whose job it is to make sure that government plays by the rules.

And what does he say? He says that when it comes to transparency, this government is . . . what's the word I'm looking for? Terrible.

He says in Ottawa, the "fog is thickening." That government is intentionally delaying or ignoring most information requests. Well, that's great news, isn't it? Just when government is preparing to spend more money than any of us could have ever imagined, it's suddenly harder to find out what they're actually up to.

Money and secrecy. What could go wrong? It's such

a good duo. It's right up there with gasoline and matches. And maybe over the last couple years, a bit of secrecy didn't really matter, because at least we knew they were spending within their limits. But now they're preparing to spend billions of dollars we don't even have. Billions, with a *B*—and like a lot of Canadians, I had a hard time wrapping my head around what a billion actually was. Then I got an email pointing out that a billion seconds ago it was 1978. Yes, a billion seconds ago, the Village People were at the top of the charts.

So a billion is a lot! And seeing as we're preparing to spend over sixty billion dollars we don't even have, maybe now is not the time for added secrecy. Or the next thing you know, we're going to wake up and find out that half that money got spent in Jim Flaherty's riding.

So if they have to spend the money, fine, but only if the fog lifts and the sun shines in.

I generally don't get nervous meeting famous people, but I was very anxious about meeting Rick Hansen. Meeting people you admire can be disappointing. Meeting someone you think of as a personal hero is a recipe for disaster . . .

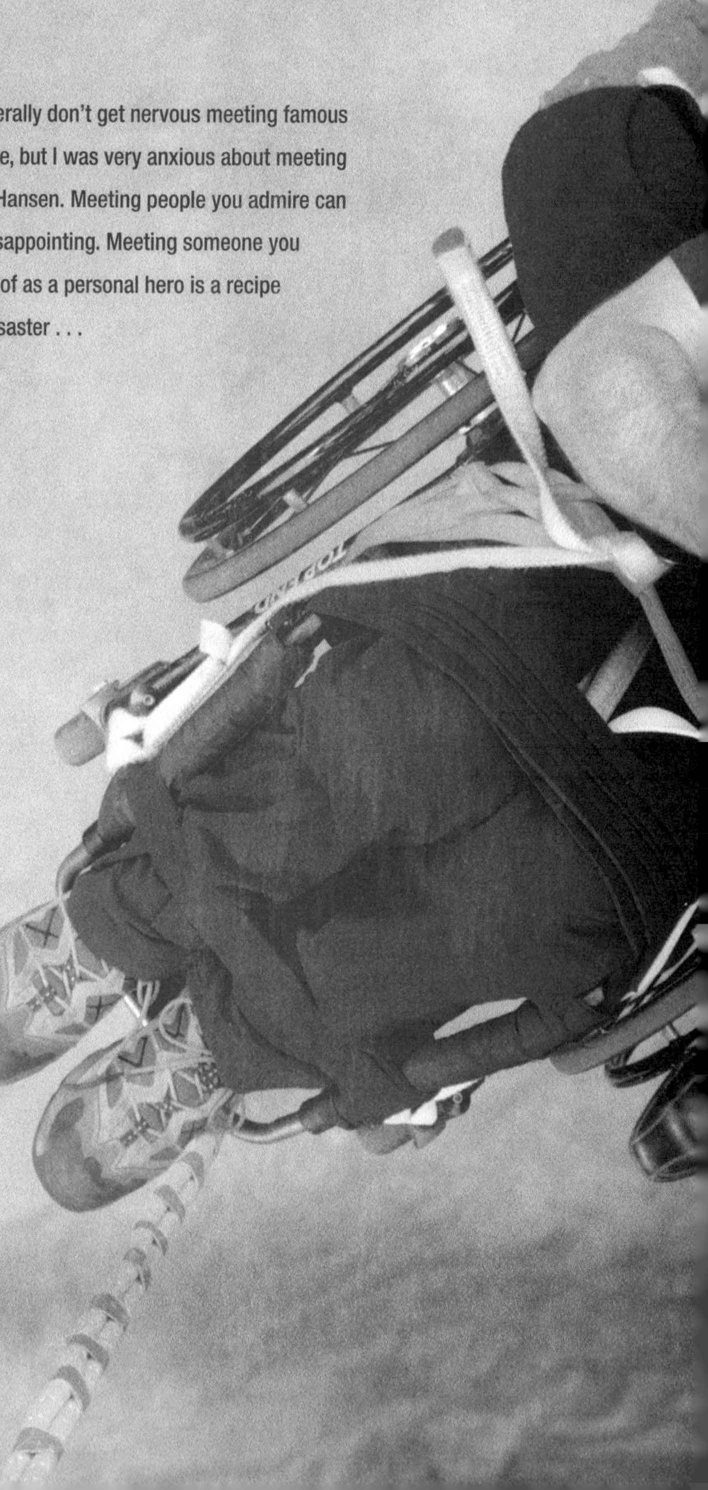

PETZL
PETZL

THE MOST SURPRISING THING about meeting Rick Hansen in person is that he can walk. He is also quite tall. You only get one chance to defy expectations completely with a first impression, and he knows how to do it.

I'd been waiting for him in a rented van on the side of a highway outside Whistler, B.C.. I didn't have to wait long as he arrived exactly on schedule, pulling up in a sporty pickup with a king cab, looking, as they say, just like himself. He opened the passenger side door, swung out his legs and stood up.

It's hard to describe my reaction. Part of me was just gobsmacked. He started moving, one leg in front of the other, along the side of the vehicle towards the back of his king cab. Part of me thought, I have a pretty big scoop on my hands. Another part of my lizard brain, the bad part, the part that admires great scams and con men, was very impressed. As far as cons go, getting in a wheelchair and circumnavigating the entire globe when you could walk the entire time is pretty spectacular.

It also crossed my mind that perhaps, somehow, he didn't know I was there watching him. Perhaps I had stumbled upon some great secret that would alter the course of my life. Suddenly, I could find myself starring in a Robert Ludlum novel, fighting for my life, being chased across the globe by trained snipers who work for the Rick Hansen Foundation. Every one of them committed to ensuring the secret would die with me.

Not so. Turns out the Man in Motion has some sort of bionic exoskeleton braces that he wears under his pants when driving around town. These braces let him get out of his truck, stand and move to the back so he can fish out his wheelchair.

I learned this later. It's a tad embarrassing to admit that the first thing I said to him was, "Holy shit. You can walk?" Awkward.

I'm not the first person to do that, apparently. He gets it all the time. When he first got the bionic exoskeleton braces, neighbours driving down the street came close to crashing thier cars into poles after seeing him upright, moving down his driveway with one hand on his truck.

That would be an ironic story to have to tell in the rehabilitation ward. "I'm in a wheelchair because I was driving down the road, saw Rick Hansen walking, lost my shit and crashed into a pole." Having met a lot of Paralympians, I've learned that they often have an epic and entertaining story to tell about how they ended up in a wheelchair. Sure, there are tragic stories, but there are also darkly funny ones. This mostly applies to men in chairs versus women. We are the stupider gender. We are the ones who get it into our heads at eighteen that it would be an excellent idea to crawl up on the garage roof and attempt a backflip onto a trampoline that will then deliver us over the fence into the neighbour's wading pool. Young women generally don't get those ideas. Young women are the ones standing on the ground, looking up, yelling, "For God's sake, Gary—don't."

This is also what allows a young man in a wheelchair to decide that nothing as insignificant as a wheelchair or a severed spinal cord is going to stop him from hurtling down a ski hill at a thousand miles an hour or taking part in the vicious sport of murderball, which has recently been renamed wheelchair rugby to make it sound less, well, murder-like.

I generally don't get nervous meeting famous people, but I was very anxious about meeting Rick Hansen. Meeting people you admire can be disappointing. Meeting someone you think of as a personal hero is a recipe for disaster. Because heroes, just like the rest of us, can be jerks or divas in person. At a benefit concert, I once watched a well-known and highly respected humanitarian berate a child volunteer because there was a baguette in his dressing room and he was on a strict wheat-free vegan diet. Four hours later, I saw the same humanitarian three sheets to the wind, sitting in the gutter, eating a sausage on a bun.

Turns out my fears about meeting Rick were totally unfounded. Not only did he avoid berating any children, but he is about as nice a guy as you could possibly meet.

I've met him now on a number of occasions, and am amazed by how generous he is with his time. Hansen is different than your standard rock star, news anchor or prime minister. People don't want to just meet Rick or get a picture with him, they want to touch him. They want to tell him exactly where they were when he rolled through their town on the Man in Motion tour. Young people, who probably don't actually remember the Man in Motion tour, want to tell him what they learned about him in school. His story has affected so many people in so many ways and they want to tell him exactly how. He greets every person in a way that is truly impressive. He is a hell of a guy. If I were prime minister, he would be my first appointment to the Senate.

Of course, I am not prime minister. Stephen Harper is, and that's why our Senate has been filling up lately with the likes of Mike Duffy, who, like Rick Hansen, can teeter short distances as long as he has something to lean on.

On that first meeting, however, I did learn something about the Man in Motion that very few people are aware of. And I'm not referring to the bionic leg braces; those, like the Prime Minister's dark mood swings, are an open secret. No, the secret about Rick Hansen, the secret he has kept hidden from his millions of admirers around the world and I am about to reveal, is this: he is afraid of heights. Despite this, he gave me the great honour of allowing me to throw him off a bridge. I admire that in a guy.

Rick came on the show to help celebrate the twenty-fifth anniversary of the Man in Motion tour. He was thrilled that I wanted to shoot an interview with him outdoors and in his province. Personally, I couldn't imagine doing a Rick Hansen shoot anywhere else, because while he is certainly a great Canadian, when I think of Rick Hansen, I think of British Columbia.

During our initial telephone conversation, I gave him my regular pitch. This is where I ask a potential guest if there is anything they do in their private life that might make for good TV. People have surprising habits, and it never hurts to ask. For example, John Baird is an amateur taxidermist—I once shot an entire interview with him on the subject of decorum in the House of Commons while he eviscerated and stuffed a raccoon, but we later bulk-erased the tape because it was far too gruesome for prime-time TV. General

Lewis MacKenzie races cars for a hobby, and my old friend General Rick Hillier does needlepoint.

Hansen told me he did have a hobby that many people were unaware of: sturgeon fishing. Wouldn't it be amazing, he said, if we went out on his boat and went fishing for sturgeon? I had opened Pandora's box. Turns out that fishing for sturgeon is not just a hobby for Hansen—he is somewhat of a sturgeon-fishing zealot. If life hadn't dealt him the blow that put him in a wheelchair, there's a good chance he would now be a world-famous sturgeon fisherman, if such a thing exists.

A few searches on YouTube taught me all I needed to know about fishing for sturgeon. It might make for a relaxing pastime, but it doesn't make for great TV. Picture it: he's in a wheelchair, on a small boat, with nowhere to go. I would be sitting in a chair next to him, with nowhere to go. We would be out in the middle of the Fraser River, bobbing up and down with our lines in the water, chatting about God knows what. My favourite TV segments involve kinetic energy, action and adventure, and I couldn't see any of that happening on a sturgeon-fishing trip. If we were lucky—a big if—one of us would get one of those butt-ugly prehistoric fish on the line and then spend so much time bringing it up from the depths that it would be about as exciting as pulling in a log.

That would be the best-case scenario.

Experience has taught me if you are going to fish on TV, you have to actually catch something or you end up looking like an idiot. When I took Bob Rae fishing, despite travelling by floatplane to the middle of pristine wilderness in northern Ontario, we didn't get a single bite. We had to take serious measures to avoid looking like idiots. And as a result, we ended up looking like naked idiots. I didn't want a repeat of that.

It was Gerald, my executive producer and partner in crime, who said about the Rick Hansen segment, "No fishing. Tell him you want to go bungee jumping."

At that point, I had no idea if a paraplegic could go bungee jumping. I knew very little about bungee jumping at all, apart from the fact that it's terrifying and dangerous. But once again, a quick search of YouTube showed me that, all over the world, guys in wheelchairs are every bit as stupid as those of us who aren't. In fact, there are piles of them who will happily pay good money to literally jump at the chance to upgrade from paraplegic to quadriplegic.

A few quick calls to some scenic British Columbia bungee-jump operations and we found one that was not only wheelchair accessible but had ample experience helping disabled individuals simulate the feeling of plunging to your death.

Now all I had to do was convince Hansen.

When I got him on the phone for our second

conversation, I could tell Rick was disappointed that I wasn't sold on sturgeon.

"Rick," I said, "how about you and I go bungee jumping?"

The silence at the other end was deafening.

He finally spoke, saying, "I would have to check with my doctor."

I can tell when someone is looking for a way out. Next, he'd be claiming there was a sudden unavoidable change in his schedule and he'd be out of town for the next year. Grasping at straws, I appealed to that part of mankind that stops them from asking directions or taking doctors' orders: "Do you always check with your doctor before you do something? What did he say about taking your wheelchair on the Great Wall of China? Was he cool when you took your wheelchair on four-lane highways?"

He admitted he rarely takes his doctor's advice and said he would get back to me. He mumbled something about heights and signed off.

I knew I'd lost him.

Lots of people are afraid of heights. My brother is afraid of heights. Growing up, my family would entertain ourselves by watching my brother, on a stepladder, trying to change a light bulb without passing out. This was back in the days when such a thing wasn't considered child abuse.

But people who are afraid of heights have a very simple way of dealing with them: they avoid them. They don't visit observation decks in the world's tallest buildings, they don't go up on their roof to install Christmas lights, and they certainly don't bungee jump.

Which is why I was taken by surprise a few days later when he called me up and said, "I'm in." I think he may have threatened my life, too, but I didn't care. I was going to meet Rick Hansen.

And just a few days later, there I was, in beautiful British Columbia, standing on a bridge with a Canadian hero. With *my* hero.

A hero I could tell was in a full-blown panic.

Not that he *said* he was in a panic, but once we got up on that bridge I could tell.

B.C. can be overwhelmingly beautiful. There are times in British Columbia when I feel like I am standing inside of a giant special effect. Can natural beauty really be this beautiful? This was one of those days. Standing on the bridge, mountains in the distance, towering trees on either side of me, I was captivated by the sight of the raging glacial river two hundred feet below. The Man in Motion, however, wasn't captivated by the river because he never once looked down. Never once did I see him peer over the edge. He would look anywhere but down.

As always, Rick caused a stir. The young men

running the bungee jump were thrilled to meet him, and this probably helped his nerves, because he went into total gentleman mode. One of the bungee technicians (are they called technicians?) was Australian and knew all about the Man in Motion. Turns out his early impressions of what Canadians were like were formed when Rick rolled through Australia twenty-five years earlier.

The bungee guys assured us that yes, they had done this before, other people in wheelchairs had made the plunge, and we were in good hands. I believed them, but part of me was thinking, Of course they would say that. I knew nothing about these people. I had no idea how long they have been on the job, or how late they were up last night, and for all I knew this Australian guy could be on the run from the law. I have done some dangerous things in my life, but this was different. I have jumped out of airplanes, for example, but in those instances I was strapped to a member of the Canadian Forces. I knew they were the best, I knew the equipment was the best, I knew they had packed the 'chute. Everything I knew about this outfit was on a glossy pamphlet. Now *I* was starting to panic.

One of the reasons why I like being with someone who is more nervous than me is that, for some reason, it alleviates my nerves. I can concentrate on helping them instead of dwelling on my own imminent death. In this case, I was also aware that the only thing worse than my bungee cord breaking would be Rick Hansen's bungee cord breaking. "Yes, Mercer's show was going great until he pushed the Canadian icon off a bridge and killed him. Ratings kind of took a hit after that."

While I was engaged in this mental horror show, John Marshall, my road director, had decided that for the purpose of the story, I would jump first. Hansen readily agreed. Don Spence, my cameraman, had only this to say: "You have to jump backwards, otherwise I can't get the shot." Backwards? Then he looked over the edge and added, "I wouldn't do that for a million dollars."

I realized a long time ago that I suffer from a psychiatric disorder common among circus folk that allows me to do things in front of an audience that I would never do if left to my own devices. There is only one circumstance where I would stand backwards on a bridge with an elastic band tied to my torso and leap into nothingness. I wouldn't do it for money and I certainly wouldn't do it for kicks. For some reason, I will do it for TV. Discuss.

They attached the cord to my body, and I looked at Rick and said, "Let's hope when this is over, you are the only guy in a wheelchair." I went to the edge, turned around and stood with only my toes on the bridge. I thought, What a beautiful day to be out fishing for sturgeon.

Advice to potential jumpers: if the plan is to count down from three and then jump, stick to the plan. I didn't. If you chicken out on your countdown, it just reveals your cowardice and makes it exponentially harder to jump when the time comes. It took me a long time to take the plunge. We counted down from three a lot. Then Rick became like some Zen master or sports psychologist and began to tell me that I could do this, that I was going to prove to myself that I could overcome adversity, that I was going to go out there and win one for the team. He's so good, I actually believed him. I counted down from three and fell backwards into nothing.

All you really think about on the way down is the bounce. You know that eventually you will reach the end of your rope. At that point, one of two things will happen: the rope will break and you will die, or it will hold and you will bounce back up from whence you came. On the way back up, a third scenario enters your mind: "What if this stupid rubber band whips me back up so hard I slam into the underside of the bridge, which from down here appears to have giant metal spikes sticking out of it? Spikes that look like they were designed to impale a TV host?" Luckily, my bungee cord held and I ricocheted up and down like a hysterical baby in one of those long-discontinued doorframe Jolly Jumpers—this is the fun part, apparently. Your brain slams against the side of your skull a few times and finally you come to a stop. By the time they dragged me back up to safety, my blood pressure was on bust and there was so much adrenaline in my bloodstream, I could have bitten my own finger off without feeling it. I looked at Rick and, drawing on all my skills gleaned from a lifetime of acting, I lied: "That's amazing," I said. "So much fun."

Now it was his turn.

So let's get this out in the open. It's not actually that straightforward for a guy in a wheelchair to bungee jump. There are a few issues. For starters, when you bungee jump, you have to jump. You have to propel yourself off the edge. You can't just drop straight down—that's dangerous. Rick can work up a wicked speed in his chair and can propel himself quite well, but to do that he needs a little room. This bridge was very narrow. This meant I would have to push him as hard as I could and kind of launch him off the edge like a Hot Wheels car.

The other issue surrounded the actual bungee cord. When an able-bodied person jumps, the cord is attached to a harness on his or her body. When someone in a wheelchair jumps, the cord has to be attached to the chair, not the person.

The bungee operator wanted Rick to feel safe, so he spoke in a very calm voice. "Okay, we are going to attach the cords here, here and here," he said, as he pointed to various points on the wheelchair and attached the cords. Rick looked dubious. "Now," said the operator, "we are going to hoist the wheelchair just a few feet in the air to show you how you will be positioned as you fall. You will be tilted back on a forty-five-degree angle. You will be comfortable. You will be like a baby in a basket."

And then they hoisted him up a few feet to show him just how safe it was. He was twelve inches off the ground when, suddenly, the wheelchair flipped ninety degrees. In the blink of an eye, his feet were in the air and his face was an inch from the platform. If it weren't for the seatbelt, he would have fallen out onto the bridge. He got a bonus adrenaline rush.

We righted him, and one of the bungee guys pointed at a part of the chair and asked me, "Do you think we should attach another cord here?"

"What the hell do I know? Why are you asking me? Ask him."

Rick said, "No, that part of the chair isn't stable."

Eventually, through trial and error, the ropes were changed. When hoisted in the air, the chair indeed tilted back slowly. It looked like it would work.

"Okay," said Hansen, "let's do this."

And so, on a count of three, I pushed with all my might and the Man in Motion flew off the edge of the bridge. He was wearing a microphone. We had to bleep some of what he said.

It's one of my favourite moments in all the years I've been on TV. It is not every day you see a guy in a wheelchair get thrown off a bridge. It's not every day you get to be the dude doing the throwing.

After his numerous residual bounces, he at last came to a stop. Dangling on the end of a rope, sun glinting on his chair, like a giant lure over the river.

"Rick, brother," I yelled. "How do you feel?"

There was a long pause, and then he answered, "I can't feel my legs!"

And his laugh echoed up the canyon.

Luckily for me and my viewers, Rick's entire *raison d'être* is to prove time and time again that a person in a wheelchair can do anything he puts his mind to. A person in a wheelchair can circle the globe, can conquer ignorance and can conquer fear. Anything an able-bodied person can do, he can do as well or better.

And thank God Rick doesn't just talk the talk; he walks the walk—or in his case, rolls the walk.

Because of that desire to lead by example, he never let something as simple as a deep-seated, ingrained fear of heights stop him from sending a message to the world. You could argue he didn't have to do that. That he's done more than his share. The Man in Motion tour was twenty-five years ago. He could easily have said, "Get some other kid in a wheelchair to throw himself off a bridge—I'm going fishing." But the Man in Motion doesn't stop moving.

Building a Habitat for Humanity house with officers and cadets of the RCMP, Regina.

Rick: "A little trick I picked up along the way: if you grunt, people think you're working hard."

BUDGET DRAMA

February 3, 2009

Like many Canadians this past week, I found myself caught up in the drama of our latest budget. Well, actually, I take that back. I watched the budget. But I was curious what our various leaders would say about our current economic crisis. And they did not disappoint. Starting with our newest political leader, Stephen Harper.

Now, I call him the newest because he seems to have been reborn. Again. I mean, here's a guy who got elected saying he was going to cut spending to the bone, and then he became the biggest-spending prime minister in Canadian history. Now he's running deficits that would make Pierre Trudeau blush. He is a no-down-payment, no-payments-forever kind of prime minister.

On his website, the Prime Minister claims that he's an economist, but I ask you, has anyone actually seen his diploma? Because this guy changes political philosophies the way the rest of us rotate our tires. What's he going do for an encore? Get a perm and join the Bloc?

And then we have the new Liberal leader, Michael Ignatieff. The budget dropped, and Iggy came out swinging. He tore the hell out of Stephen Harper, and that budget, in a truly spectacular display of withering criticism. Pausing only long enough to say, "Oh, by the way, we will be supporting this budget completely."

We've seen that act from a Liberal leader before. The only difference is, this time around we actually knew what he was saying.

And then, poor old Jack Layton. He seems to be in the middle of a psychological crisis triggered by the fact that he thought he was going to be in cabinet and now it's never going to happen. It's a sin, really. He's like that fellow in Ontario who thought he'd won the Lotto, only to find out his ticket had a typo.

And then, to make matters worse, nobody even cared what Jack had to say because Jack had already announced that he would vote against the budget long before he knew what was in the budget. It's what we call a case of premature enunciation.

At that point in the proceedings, I couldn't help but wonder what the security guard in the foyer of the House of Commons would do to save our economy. Because right now, based on what the other three have said, he's got my vote.

BEST BEHAVIOUR

February 24, 2009

Unlike, it seems, everyone else in the country, I was not looking forward to Barack Obama's visit. Now, don't get me wrong—I was thrilled that he decided to come to Canada. I was just nervous. You know what it's like. We've all been there. You've got people coming over, you want to make a good impression, but what if something goes wrong? What if someone says the wrong thing? What if the guest of honour is allergic to caribou and goes into anaphylactic shock? You just can't control these things.

And remember, this visit was on Parliament Hill. What if there was a glitch in security and somehow Obama ended up on an elevator with Mike Duffy—or, God forbid, an actual cabinet minister? You only get one chance to make a first impression.

But everyone rose to the occasion, from the crowds on Parliament Hill, which were amazing, to our political leaders. Look at Stephen Harper—clearly, Obama brings out the best in him. He never stopped smiling. He never broke out the dead-eye stare once. Hell, he was so excited, he went on CNN and said that he was glad that Bush was out of the White

House because it was Bush that was stopping Harper from fighting climate change. Think about that. Stephen Harper on Wolf Blitzer sounding like David Suzuki. Clearly, change is possible. If this keeps up, next thing you know, dogs will have kittens.

And then there's Michael Ignatieff. He got a fifteen-minute audience with Obama, and what did he do? He brought Bob Rae. Now, that's a very classy move. Until recently, these men were bitter rivals. That's like calling up someone who tried to steal your date and saying, "Hey, just to show you there's no hard feelings—I've got two playoff tickets. Why don't you come along?"

And then, of course, there was Jack Layton—nowhere to be seen. His finest performance in years.

Overall, a very good day on Parliament Hill. This is a unique moment in time, though. Obama won't be this popular forever. Fame is fleeting, but let's hope the spectacle of politicians acting honourably won't be.

Flying with the ice pilots of Buffalo Air in Yellowknife, North West Territories. Temperature: minus 40.

Rick: "I can barely move—that's my challenge today. I've got so many layers, and then with the snow pants and boots and the jacket and the layers . . ."

Ice pilot: "It's not really about the layers. It's about how smart you are when you're outside."

Rick: "Then I'm done. They'll just find my corpse, and that will be the end of the piece."

NOBODY WANTS AN ELECTION

The Globe and Mail, *September 25, 2009*

He could have been anywhere from 50 to 65, he has worked his entire life on container ships in the St. Lawrence Seaway, and he put three daughters through university. He has at different times in his life voted for three different parties, and standing on a wharf in Lunenburg, N.S., he told me that, if there is an election this fall, he is going to do something he has never done.

He's staying home.

He summed up our current crop of political leaders this way: "If all three of them were in the water, I'd be hard-pressed not to watch them drown."

And he happened to mention he goes to church on Sundays.

This is not a man who is suffering from voter apathy; this is a hungry man with a seafood allergy, looking at the menu from Red Lobster.

For years now, after every election, faced with increasingly dismal turnouts, journalists and pundits ask the same questions: Why are Canadian voters staying home? What is wrong with us?

Maybe it's time to ask not what is wrong with Canadians, but what is wrong with our leaders. Or better yet, let's just start placing the blame squarely at their feet.

It's not like we choose the leaders, the parties do. And apparently this is as good as it gets. No wonder people are apathetic. Elections aren't the problem, our choices are.

It may be a myth that the Inuit have 100 different words to describe snow; it is an absolute truth that people on Parliament Hill have twice as many words to describe Stephen Harper's various levels of angry.

We have a minority government that bombards us, practically year-round, with campaign-style ads that are more vitriolic and personal than anything ever witnessed in Canadian history.

When it comes to issues that Canadians care about—the economy, Afghanistan, heath care, medical isotopes—there is a campaign of misinformation that qualifies as pathological. When asked the philosophy behind our Prime Minister's communication strategy, Mr. Harper's former campaign manager, Tom Flanagan, summed it up with the phrase: "It doesn't have to be true; it just has to be plausible."

Parents of Canada, make sure you impart that little nugget to your kids before they head out to school on Monday.

Voting Conservative is not a problem for a majority of Canadians; we've done it before. Voting for an angry guy who thinks we're stupid and will believe anything? That takes some getting used to.

Voting Liberal is certainly not a problem for a majority of Canadians, either. In fact, the federal Liberals got so used to the notion that Canadians would dutifully elect them, they forgot that any other scenario was possible. For Liberals victory was just something that happened 40-odd days after an election was called; much in the same way the rest of us are fairly confident that the sun will rise tomorrow.

The Liberals should have a bit of an advantage this time around. Having been beaten badly in the last election, they quickly took Stéphane Dion out behind the barn and he hasn't been seen since. Immediately afterward, there was a puff of white smoke and the Liberal party suddenly had a brand new leader in Michael Ignatieff. He is by all accounts highly qualified, having dazzled many people at dinner parties for decades.

Michael Ignatieff is, as we speak, surrounded by a brigade of young people in pointy shoes and designer glasses who work for him, worship him and Twitter about him. Why should we vote for him? I've read the tweets; I've yet to see an answer.

Those of us who view politics in part as a blood sport believe that in the last election, Stéphane Dion made the classic error of bringing a knife to a gunfight.

At least he showed up. So far, Ignatieff is hiding in the woods. Literally.

In the TV ads launched to counterpunch the Tories, we are treated to the image of Michael Ignatieff, alone among the trees, free associating. His message, if I remember it correctly, is about the importance of ensuring that tomorrow's green jobs of today fuel yesterday's growth now. I think he might mention China, too.

If that's the best he can do, his next trip to the woods is going to involve a shovel and a bag of lime.

And then there's Jack Layton. NDP leader Jack Layton closes out his party's national convention with a keynote speech on Sunday, August 17.

Canadians have never come close to electing a New Democrat government federally, and yet Jack dreams. This is fine, as dreams are important.

The problem with Jack is, we all saw how excited he got when he actually thought that he was going to be a part of a coalition government. It wasn't a normal excitement; it was the kind of excitement that scares other passengers on a plane.

I don't know if this is what has turned off my friend on the Lunenburg wharf, but it's a definite possibility. Ours wasn't a long conversation, which is surprising. Normally, when confronted with someone who justifies not voting, I have an entire arsenal at my disposal.

I'm a guy who has advocated mandatory voting. I have always believed in my heart of hearts we would be a far better country if everyone were obligated to take twenty minutes out of their life on Election Day to mark an *X*.

That said, I can't help but feel great sympathy for someone who just happens to be standing on a wharf contemplating the fact that it's hard to imagine voting for someone when you can't even wrap your head around throwing them a rope.

COME OUT SWINGING, PLEASE

September 29, 2009

I'm a little disappointed that there's no election. Not because I think there should be an election; I just like watching them as a blood sport. And like all fight fans, I always hope that the next fight is going to be better than the last.

Let's face it: the last election was over about thirty seconds into the first round. It was Harper's right from the start.

If the Inuit have a hundred different words to describe snow, there are at least twice as many words to describe Stephen Harper's various levels of angry. If he doesn't like you, he's going hurt you. And if you trust the polls, about 35 percent of Canadians like it rough. So maybe the guy's onto something.

The Liberals went out and got themselves Michael Ignatieff, which was very exciting for about five minutes. Since then, basically, he's been hiding in the woods—or at least that's what his TV ads seem to indicate. He's out there now, as we speak, rambling around, free associating, talking about how tomorrow's green jobs of today must fuel yesterday's growth now. This guy can't fight; he can barely make a fist.

Michael. Smarten up. You're about to go into the ring with Mike Tyson. He's going to bite you.

And as for Jack Layton, it's not like he doesn't know how to fight. Jack's problem is the minute things start looking good, like when he thought that he was actually going to be part of a coalition, he gets all excited, and not excited in a good way, either.

So really, from a spectator's point of view, maybe it's a good thing we're not going to the polls. If for no other reason than that I want them all to refocus and, when the bell rings, to come out swinging. Because after all, if we're going to pay $350 million to watch this go down, let's make it a good show.

A private tour of Rideau Hall with Governor General David Johnston.

Rick: "You are the Queen's representative on earth here in Canada."

GG: "That is correct."

Rick: "So you are she."

GG: "Well, in a sense . . ."

Rick: "I should straighten up. God sakes here, I'm talking to the Queen."

GG: "You're straight enough, thank you very much."

Rick: "Well, okay . . ."

VEGETABLES AND PRIMATES

October 6, 2009

So, big goings on in the House of Commons this past week. The Liberals tabled a straightforward non-confidence motion. If it had passed the entire minority government would have collapsed. Now this may not seem like a big deal but it is. It's only happened twice since Confederation. So I can't help but think that some time in the future—I mean, hundreds of years from now—some academic will study the official record of what was said and done in the House of Commons this week and come to the conclusion that in October 2009, Canada was governed by monkeys.

Starting with the Liberals. It was their motion. It was their job to get up in the House and explain why this government should fall. So up pops Michael Ignatieff. And to be fair, for the first time ever, he laid out what he would do differently if he were prime minister. Fascinating stuff. Problem is, he never really got around to the "Why the government should fail" part, which is the only reason we were watching in the first place.

And then it was the government's turn to respond. For this, they chose that great parliamentarian John

Baird. And did John Baird get up and say why they should survive? No. Instead, John Baird stood up in the House of Commons and accused Michael Ignatieff, in front of all of Canada, of owning a condominium in Toronto, that—wait for it—has a balcony. So if you're one of the two million Canadians who live in a condo with a balcony, be warned: John Baird and the Conservative Party do not condone your lifestyle.

And then there was the NDP, who did not act like monkeys. To say so would be insulting to monkeys. Because when it came time to vote, Jack Layton and the NDP, who held the balance of power, did nothing. They abstained. If the entire NDP caucus had been replaced with thirty-six turnips, the results would have been exactly the same. And so, at the end of the day, the government survived. The vegetables and the primates, they lived to serve yet another day.

And for anyone who happened to tune in for the action, cheer up. Because, really, after a week like this, there's nowhere to go but up.

HOW COULD HE HAVE KNOWN?

October 13, 2009

There was really only one story in Ottawa last week. The champagne corks that were popping out of the Prime Minister's Office could be seen from outer space. Stephen Harper has hit the magic 40-percent approval rating, which means a majority government is now within his grasp.

What I find astounding is that the Tories attribute this success not to his piano playing but to his economic record. This is confusing to me because it implies that somewhere it's been recorded that he's doing a good job. I mean, let's not forget, this is the same prime minister who, twelve months ago, told us we could never go into a deficit because there could be no recession as long as he was in charge.

Now, of course, hindsight is 20/20. Which is why, if you ask Tories about what Harper said, they all say the same thing. They say, "Ah . . . well . . . please . . . How could he have known we were in a recession?" Well, he could have read a newspaper, or asked my mother, or spoken to a cab driver, but I guess, barring that, they're right. He just didn't see it coming. So instead, we went from zero to the largest deficit in Canadian history. Sixty billion dollars in one year alone.

The good news is that the same guy who said we could never go into a deficit now says we will pay off that $60 billion without raising taxes or cutting spending.

Imagine for a moment your fiancé comes home and tells you that when you weren't looking, he or she dropped 150 grand that you don't have at the casino. Now imagine that the same fiancé says, "Don't worry. We'll pay it back without making a single change to our lifestyle . . . I stand on my financial record." I think, piano playing or not, we'd all start looking at other options.

Now, don't get me wrong—just to be clear to my Tory friends, I am not saying that I believe Michael Ignatieff is better suited to manage this economy. I'm saying that, based on the past twelve months, Porky Pig is better suited to manage this economy.

As it stands right now, this country has a $60 billion wake-up call coming, and for the record, not a single leader has come even close to being honest.

Carriage racing at the High Country Carriage Driving Club, Calgary.

Rick: "This is your team outfit? And I know I should look like an athlete, but I feel like I should be selling stolen electronics out of the trunk of a car."

FLU CONFUSION

October 20, 2009

I cannot begin to tell you how confused I am about the swine flu. Every day brings different reports, conflicting advice. All I know is, at this point, I swear to God I'm 80 percent hand sanitizer. Whenever I run into one of those Purell pumps, I ride that lever like I'm a senior citizen at Casino Rama. I go to a bar, I order Purell and Coke. Does it help? I have no idea. But I do know that the minute you're all cleaned up and disinfected, you get in the elevator and some dude comes along and coughs on your neck. And that can't be good.

So, if you're like me, you probably have some questions. You, too, might have been tempted to go onto the Health Canada website to see what they're saying about the swine flu. If you haven't yet gone to that website, my advice to you is: don't. Unless, of course, you're doing research on how to bore, panic and confuse people all at the same time.

The first thing you have to know about the federal government's swine flu website: they spelled *coughs* wrong. Six million dollars they spent; they don't have spell check. They also say everyone, without exception, should get the swine flu vaccine. Then they say, "Don't worry, we currently have a million vaccines stockpiled." That's great, except for the fact that there are thirty-five million Canadians. Unless we're looking for the miracle of the loaves and fishes here, this means I have to strangle thirty-four people on the way to my clinic.

Although, who am I kidding? I live in a riding represented by the NDP. I ain't seeing no vaccine. Meanwhile, if you live in Jim Flaherty's riding, you get three vaccines plus a giant novelty cheque for five grand.

Some people may say that I'm being cynical. I'm not. I'm being practical. While the federal government is busy spreading confusion, it's our job to spread nothing. All we can do is wash our hands, cough into our sleeves, and for God's sake, stay off the Internet.

THE SHOVELS ARE OUT

October 27, 2009

It seems like only yesterday the federal government was rolling out its economic stimulus program. And now, ten months later, the shovels are at work, but they're not shovelling dirt. Conservative ridings are getting way more money than anyone else. And when asked about this, the Prime Minister simply shrugs and says, with all the conviction in the world, "It's just not true." He's like one of those people who, when confronted with all the evidence to the contrary, will insist that the earth is flat or that John Baird is funny.

Not all the Tories are so good. My favourite is Tony Clement. For the last ten months, Tony's been driving around his riding, wearing a giant gold hat and throwing our money out the window. And I love when he has to stand up and defend himself in the House of Commons because—and Tony should take this as a compliment—he's a terrible liar. Every time he answers a question, he looks like a ten-year-old who just got caught stealing change out of Mom's purse.

I'm not saying this is anything new. This was invented by Sir John A. Macdonald. It was practised by Lester Pearson. It was polished by Brian Mulroney.

It was perfected by Jean Chrétien. But Stephen Harper has turned it into an art form. He is the Yo-Yo Ma of pork-barrel politics.

And it's not just about pavement with this guy, either. Consider this: as part of the stimulus funding there's a $45 million "accessibility" fund. This is money for disabled people. Ninety-two percent of that money has gone to Conservative ridings.

Boy, when he promised a transparent government, he wasn't kidding. He's downright see-through.

Yes, the emperor has no clothes, but he does have wheelchair ramps, and if you didn't vote right, you don't get one.

DON'T PANIC

November 3, 2009

Well, there's no doubt about it. At this point in time, it's clear: this country is under attack by a highly contagious virus. And I'm not talking about the swine flu here—we've got a vaccine for that. I'm talking about good, old-fashioned fear. I've never seen anything like it. This past week, we had thousands of people lining up outside a clinic for five hours when they were told there was no vaccine inside. Do you know who lines up for five hours in the cold? Thirteen-year-olds looking for Jonas Brothers tickets. Rational adults do not do that. And it's not even our fault. Canadians are terrified. And in times of crisis, we get our information from the media and the government. Which is ironic, because we don't trust either one of them. And look at the media. Last week, every time you turned on the news, the anchor was saying, "Oh my God, there's an outbreak at a Toronto hospital. Outbreak, outbreak outbreak!" And then they happen to mention, "Oh, by the way, 'outbreak' is a technical term. It means three people have the flu."

No, no, no, no. We know what "outbreak" is. It's a Dustin Hoffman movie about a monkey that bites a dude and then his head explodes. In fact, it's two and half hours of a guy's head exploding. So the media's not really helping us out on the whole panic front.

And then there's the government. Sure, it would be nice if the government stepped up to the plate, but to be fair, they are very busy coming up with advertisements telling us what a great job they're doing with the whole shovels-in–the-ground thing. Apparently, you can only advertise so many things at once. So it looks like we're on our own. But that's okay, because Canadians can beat this thing. All we have to do is put our minds to it. Because unlike the flu, panic is all in our head.

Whale watching in the Bay of Fundy with opera star Measha Brueggergosman.

Rick: "You know what's a shame? That you lost 160 pounds, and then you came on this show and we made you wear this."

Measha: "I know. It adds volume, I won't lie."

Rick: "The camera adds ten pounds, and then the survival suit adds about twenty-five."

HEIR TODAY

November 17, 2009

So the future King of Canada, Prince Charles, and his wife, Camilla, have left our shores and returned safely home to Britain. And sticking with that long-held Canadian tradition of absolute politeness, practised at dinner parties all over this great land, we can talk freely now that the guests of honour have finally left.

Thank God that's over with. Why is it when the Royals pop in for a visit, we're expected to drop everything? And we do—the Prime Minister of Canada, the Governor General, all the TV networks. In fact, the only people who didn't show up this time were the crowds.

This royal visit began in an empty stadium in St. John's, Newfoundland, and went downhill from there. And believe me, if the Royal Family can't fill a stadium in Newfoundland, a place where some people still fly the Union Jack, there's a serious problem. The Tragically Hip can fill that room four nights in a row, and they charge admission.

I know what's going on here. Canada is the "B" circuit. It's just like when I was a kid, and the World

Wrestling Federation said they were coming to town. Did they send the Macho Man, Randy Savage? No, instead they sent some drunk guy in tights named Gary.

That's the way the Royal Family views Canada. Look at Prince Harry. There's a superstar. They sent Prince Harry to Lesotho for two and a half months. And what do we get? Eleven days with Camilla and a bill for a couple million bucks.

Look, Canada is 142 years old, and we still pledge allegiance to a family that lives in a castle in England. No hard feelings, nothing personal. It's time we grew up.

DELIVER US FROM THIS GARBAGE

November 24, 2009

It goes without saying that members of Parliament have certain privileges that the rest of us do not. And that's as it should be. After all, these are honourable citizens who answered a higher calling to represent the needs and wants of their constituents, and they would rather die than waste our money or disrespect the office. Or is it the other way around? I get confused.

Anyway, they've got special privileges. One of which is, they can send mail-outs and fliers all over this country and we get to pick up the tab. Which is great, because one of the things that all Canadians can agree on is that we love junk mail. The only thing we like better than junk mail is really offensive junk mail that we paid for.

If the Tories send you a flier saying the Liberals are all anti-Jewish, you paid for that. If the Liberals send you a flier saying the Tories sent body bags to northern Indian reservations to deal with the swine flu, you paid for that. If Olivia Chow sends you a flier saying—well, God knows what it said, because, let's face it, you threw it in the blue bin the minute it arrived, you paid for that. How this helps the democratic process, I have no idea. I ask you, how many more trees have to die so Stephen Harper can warn us once again that Michael Ignatieff taught at Harvard? Yes, we know, he taught at an American university. Clearly, he's a very bad man.

But never mind the trees. Last year, MPs from all political parties spent over $10 million on these mail-outs. Ten million dollars a year. Hey everyone, I've got an idea. Let's save ourselves $10 million. No one in Ottawa has mentioned this, or even seems to care, but as of last week, Canada's debt is half a trillion dollars. The least they can do is stop adding to it by sending us garbage. In words and paper.

HOW TO USE AN ESCALATOR

December 1, 2009

Every now and then, an issue comes along that transcends politics, that transcends all socio-economic realities. And sometimes the truth needs to be said, no matter how painful that truth may be to some people. This is one of those times, and this is it.

Just because you are on an escalator, that does not mean you have to stop walking.

Up or down, it is an escalator; it is not a ride at Canada's Wonderland. It was designed to keep people moving faster. Which is why it's called an escalator not a slowthingsdown-alator. And if you must stop on an escalator—because you've got bad knees or you're just a much calmer person then me—you have to stay to the right. The left lane is a passing lane. That means you cannot put your shopping bag there. That also means your best friend cannot park there and talk to you about why you really should have bought that blouse at Value Village. Do you know why? Because when you do that, everyone behind you wants to kill you. And I only bring this up because I am a calm and rational person, but I if I ever go to prison it will be because of something that happened on an escalator. Either that, or near the front doors of a shopping mall or an airport.

Okay, we all know that sometimes big buildings are overwhelming. That does not mean that you get to walk through the front door and just stop and look around for three minutes. If you need to get your bearings, the rules of the road apply here. You must pull over. Find a wall—you can spend all the time you want over there. And while we're on the subject, if you get in an elevator before letting people off an elevator, that should be a criminal offence. With mandatory sentencing.

I don't know why they don't teach this stuff in schools.

Look, we are heading into the holiday season, people. There are going to be big crowds, it's stressful enough. "Peace and goodwill" is the standard wish for the season; that's only going to happen if everyone keeps moving.

At the Canadian Western Agribition, Regina.

Rick: "If you are in the market for a bison, a heifer, a calf or a goat, this is the place to be. They also do excellent beef on a bun."

Bull: "*Bellowwwww.*"

LOAN SHARKS

January 12, 2010

The holidays are over and everyone is back to work. Everyone, that is, except for members of Parliament. Because as we all know, the Prime Minister has decided to suspend Parliament so we can all focus on the Olympics. I believe that Canadians will focus on the Olympics, but only when the Olympics actually happen. In over a month's time.

For the time being, Canadians are focused on one thing and one thing only. Our credit card bills. If you don't believe me, Prime Minister, ask your chef or your driver. They will tell you.

There I was this week, looking at my Visa bill, and I felt like the dude from *The Da Vinci Code,* looking at the parchment, trying to decipher what exactly happened over the holidays. And then I wondered, What kind of interest rate are they charging me here?

So I get out the magnifying glass—the really powerful one I have lying around in case I want to examine some protozoa. And I saw in the very fine print that my interest rate is 20 percent. Twenty percent. Do you know who else charges 20 percent interest to borrow money in this country? Loan sharks.

Now, I'm not advocating that anyone go to a loan shark. If you're going to borrow money from the criminal element, you might as well stick with one of Canada's five major banks. But there is a serious problem when a guy named Larry the Fence offers a lower interest rate than MasterCard.

My New Year's resolution is to avoid cards. All cards. At this point, I'm this close to getting a tattoo across my forehead that says, "No, I don't have an Optimum card, and no, I don't collect Air Miles." All I want to do is buy some shampoo and not pay 20 percent interest. And focus on the Olympics.

TORIES PLUNGE IN POLLS

January 19, 2010

How about those polls? For the first time in a very long time, the Liberals and the Tories are essentially tied, at least within the margin of error. Now, polls never tell the full story, but this much is certain: whenever the party in power drops fifteen points in fifteen days, you can be sure of one thing—someone in charge just did something really stupid.

In this case, the Prime Minister figured he could suspend Parliament for three months and get away with it, because, in his words, Canadians just don't care. Boy, was he wrong. Wow. He should get out more. Maybe go to a Tim Hortons. Get a feel for the place.

This is what I love about Canada. Yes, we are apathetic. But the minute anyone tries to use our apathy against us, suddenly we start to care big time. It's strange that the Prime Minister doesn't get this. Instead, he just keeps saying, "Oh, don't worry. Yes, I've suspended Parliament, but don't worry, I'm hard at work."

You know what? Big deal. Of course he's at work—he's the Prime Minister. I'm sure Raul Castro's going to put in a full day tomorrow running Cuba. We just like to think that in Canada, the bar is set a little bit higher.

Bottom line is, Canadians got together, we elected 308 members of Parliament to go to Ottawa and represent us, and one member of Parliament, Stephen Harper, sent them packing.

Prime Minister, with all due respect, I know it's your job to run the country. I'm glad you're hard at it. But it's the voters who get to send MPs home. And with polls numbers like this, you might want to keep that in mind.

POLITICAL PROPS

January 26, 2010

Canadians have been very generous to Haiti. People in this country have given an incredible amount of money. But once again, it's members of the Canadian Forces that are doing the heavy lifting. Because really, by the time most of us realized just how devastating this situation was, by the time most of us sat down at our laptops and made a donation, a thousand Canadian soldiers were already on their way to Haiti.

And a thousand more show up this week. Imagine if that was your job: just drop everything and go to hell on earth with no idea when you'll be coming home to your family. I don't know what it's like where you work, but people at the CBC complain when the elevator's on the fritz. But that's soldiers for you. That's what they do. And that's why we admire them.

And that is why soldiers make the perfect political props. In the old days, politicians loved to get their pictures taken with babies. These days, it's soldiers. Which is why, this past July, three hundred Canadian soldiers were given a mission. They were told to drop everything and show up at Canadian Forces

Base Gagetown, in uniform, in front of the cameras, and clap and cheer as the Minister of Defence announced that this government was finally buying them new armoured vehicles, which we know they so desperately need.

And so it was perfect timing this past week, when every headline was dominated by the humanitarian crisis in Haiti, that the government let it slip out very quietly that the purchase of armoured vehicles is now on "permanent hold," or what a civilian would call "cancelled." Turns out it was just a photo op, and perhaps a new low in Canadian politics.

You know, it's one thing for the government to order soldiers to put their lives at risk for Canada. That's their job. But to drag them out and use them as a political prop, that's going too far.

At least babies can scream or throw up on a politician. Soldiers, they don't get that option.

Marching in the Santa Claus Parade, Toronto.

Ron Barbaro (he's on the left): "God, you can't get good clowns these days."

AN ASSAULT ON US ALL

February 2, 2010

For Stephen Harper, a good cabinet minister is like a well-behaved child from the fifties. They should be seen and not heard, minus the seen part. Which is why the first time most of us heard there was a woman named Gail Shea in cabinet was when a woman from New York decided to smack her in the face with a tofu pie.

Being a member of Parliament is bad enough. It's not like the job comes with a lot of respect. Those days are long gone. Most people would rather see their kids go into a life of air conditioner repair than politics. But the bottom line is, we elect these people, and when we do, we expect them to be accessible to the public. That's their job. And if we don't like them, there are plenty of ways to protest that are actually effective.

Hell, so many people protested against Stephen Harper last week the man is in full-blown panic mode. He's out there as we speak, running around, saying that his brand new legacy is going to be protecting women and children in the Third World. All of a sudden, he sounds like Bono.

But that's the way our system works. We can yell, we can scream, we can protest, we can throw the bums out—but no touching. Everyone in this country—with the exception of hockey players, apparently—has the right to go to work and not get a smack in the face. Members of Parliament are no exception. We elect them, they serve at our pleasure, and if someone assaults them, it's an assault on all of us.

So to the woman from New York, who decided to leave her country and come to *our* country to assault a member of our Parliament, welcome to Canada. I hope you like prison food and that you bought a one-way ticket.

HERE'S TO TEAM CANADA

February 9, 2010

Some people see the glass as half empty, other people see the glass as half full. I see the glass and blame the Prime Minister. I'm what you might call a cynic. I can be cynical about anything, even the lead-up to the Olympics.

Not that it was hard. In certain Ottawa circles, it's been a parlour game to sit around guessing how many medals our Olympians have to win in order to guarantee this government a majority. Mother Teresa would become cynical listening to that.

But that said, once the Games begin later this week, I am in. For starters, the entire world is going to freak when they see how beautiful Vancouver is. See, we forget, we take this for granted, but British Columbia, that's one sexy-looking province. Seriously, I expect some Germans' heads will pop right off. Japanese, too.

And then there are the athletes. Really, it's all about them—the 206 members of Team Canada.

Now, I'm very lucky. I have a job where I've got to meet a lot of Olympians and a lot of Paralympians. But even if I live to be a thousand, I will never understand these people. I have never, in my entire life, come close to being as committed to a single thing as they are to their sports. And God knows, they don't do it for the money. Most of them still live under the poverty line. They work harder than anyone I have ever met in my life, and they do it because they love their sports and they love their country. It can make the most committed cynic believe the glass is half full.

So, with just days to go before the opening of the 2010 Winter Games in Vancouver, here's to the members of Team Canada. You own the podium already.

OLYMPIAN INSPIRATION

March 2, 2010

When Kaillie Humphries was just six years old, she saw Mark Tewksbury win a gold medal in the swimming pool and was inspired to be an Olympian. Eighteen years later, she got in a bobsled and won gold on a mountain. That is a legacy of Canadian Olympians. And boy, did we ever meet a great bunch this time around. Alexander Bilodeau, Clara Hughes, Tessa Virtue and Scott Moir, Joannie Rochette . . . the list goes on and on. All amazing Canadians.

But now that the Olympics are over, all of these athletes are worried that the funding for amateur sport is going to dry up. And you know what? They should be. Because so far, all signs out of Ottawa seem to indicate that the minute that flame goes out, the tap's getting turned off.

And as we've been told, it's a mighty big tap. Huge amounts of money are involved. And this is the thing about governments—they can take any amount of money and make it seem like a lot or a little. This government, this wonderful government, has told us over and over again that it has spent over $55 million over five years supporting amateur athletes. What a huge amount of money. Who's ever heard of such a sum?

Fifty-five million over five years. In fact, it's the same amount of money this same government has spent in one year, in one Conservative riding, preparing for one G8 meeting. A meeting, by the way, that will last one day. Starts at nine, ends at five. And at the end of the day, the only Canadian on a podium will be the Prime Minister. Never mind owning the podium—this is more like pass the Imodium.

My guess is that when the meeting's done, no six-year-old is going to be inspired to be the best in the world at anything. That is the job of our Olympians. Team Canada did their job; now it's time we do ours. And make sure the bucks don't stop here.

RMR

THRONE OFF

March 9, 2010

Usually, I love a Speech from the Throne. As far as politics go, it's pure show business. Everyone gets dressed up. There's an actual throne for the Governor General and a little tiny chair for the Prime Minister to curl up in. And the whole thing starts when a dude in a funny hat marches up the hall and bangs on the door with an ebony rod topped with a golden lion.

It all went downhill after that. For starters, it went on forever. *Avatar* was shorter. Now, maybe it was the

With Kyle Shewfelt at the Olympic Oval, Calgary.

Rick: "You broke two legs."

Kyle: "I broke *both* my legs . . . yeah."

Rick: "Broke both your legs. And then you went on to compete in the Olympics."

Kyle: "Yes."

Rick: "Which is incredible. And a lot of that had to do with your good outlook, don't you think? I emailed you probably within hours of hearing you'd broken your legs, and I remember you emailed me back the next day, and you were so positive and so convinced you were going to go on and compete in the Olympics. And I remember thinking, *The pills he's on!*"

anticipation. After all, the Prime Minister closed down government for three months so he could "recalibrate." Sometimes it's hard to live up to the hype. When this happens in Hollywood, they bring in experts at the last minute to insert some sex and violence to distract the audience. Unfortunately, you can't just insert a car chase in a Throne Speech, so the Tories did the next best thing: they announced the creation of—wait for it—Seniors' Day.

Now, that's good government! Because as we know, the greatest problem facing senior citizens on a fixed income in this country is that they don't have a day. Like, you know, secretaries do. And then, how about that twist at the halfway point? The government announced the creation of a new award for volunteers called the Prime Minister's Award, featuring—wait for it—the Prime Minister. How sexy is that?

And then, of course, the climax of the entire piece—they anounced that they wanted to rewrite the lyrics to "O Canada" to appeal to more women. Well, that went over really well, didn't it? Especially in a week where the minister in charge of the status of women, Helena Guergis, is so far off the rails she's not allowed within a hundred feet of an airport, let alone an open microphone.

So there you have it. They had three months to prepare, and the best they came up with was Seniors

Day and a Prime Minister's Award, and the only thing they tried to recalibrate was the national anthem. An idea that lasted two days. That's not a Speech from the Throne; that's a cry for help.

WHO YOU KNOW

March 16, 2010

A very wise man once said that the secret to success in politics is sincerity—and if you can fake that, you've got it made. On the flipside, if people ever get the idea that you're saying one thing and then doing another, you're a dead man walking. Which is why my guess is the Tories wish they could start this month all over again.

First up, we had Jim Flaherty's tough new budget. Jim announced we were all going to have to make huge sacrifices and tighten our belts—and then he led by example by sneaking out the back door, getting in a private government jet and flying to London, Ontario, so he could get his picture taken at Tim Hortons. Do as I say, people, not as I do!

And then we find out that hidden inside this tough, cost-cutting budget is an extra $13 million a year for the Prime Minister's own Privy Council Office. That's an extra quarter of a million dollars a week for the PMO. Talk about your sacrifices.

And then there's the ongoing Helena Guergis saga, which I don't understand. I mean, does she have pictures of the Prime Minister in a dress or something?

This is a prime minister who has spent millions of dollars collecting stupid things his enemies have said and then mailing them out all over Canada, and yet Helena Guergis screams that Prince Edward Island is a hellhole at the top of her lungs and that's just fine with him. And then she doesn't even apologize. She releases a written statement. Try that one, kids. Next time your parents tell you to apologize for something, don't do it in person, no, just have someone type something up and then fax it over in the morning.

Actually, don't bother—it won't work. Unless you're a cabinet minister or you're married to one, and then normal rules don't apply.

As always, if you want to get away with something in this country, it's not what you know, it's who you know in the PMO.

WEBCAM 'EM

March 23, 2010

Canada's twenty-second prime minister, Stephen Harper, did something truly historic this past week. He did something that no Canadian prime minister had ever done before. He went on YouTube and answered questions.

Now, granted, by YouTube standards he's not as popular as, say, a cat that can flush the toilet, but the fact is he embraced the new media, and for that he should be commended. Because I believe now, more than ever, that it is the Internet that can help save Canadian democracy. And it needs saving. And not from any outside forces, but from the people we have so tragically elected. Because believe me, they're out of control.

Kids on field trips go into Question Period, having learned in school that democracy is something worth dying for. They leave an hour later convinced that blithering idiots rule the world. And can you blame them? Anyone who has watched Question Period live knows the evidence is on display. The problem is, Canadians at home can't see that, because all of the bad behaviour is hidden off camera. And the solution is webcams. Regular, old-fashioned webcams, the same kind of webcams that many of our younger members of Parliament, like Pierre Poilievre or Jason Kenney, probably have in their homes. There should be one on every desk in the House of Commons. And the minute that place opens up, those cameras should be on.

And we should be able to go online, click and watch our member of Parliament. You know, kind of like a fancy baby monitor. If they're missing in action, like Michael Ignatieff was all last week, we should be able to stare at the empty seat and come to our own conclusions. If they want to sit there and twitter about who's wearing what, like Lisa Raitt, or just sit there and bark like a rabid dog, like John Baird does when he's in a good mood, we should be able to watch that, too.

Believe me, after one week of webcamming, they will be on their best behaviour. And who knows, maybe something might even get done.

Because nothing inspires a politician to greatness like a good old-fashioned shaming.

Volunteering at the Humane Society, Charlottetown, P.E.I.

Rick: "I actually have fond memories of being dewormed as a child. Seriously. The kids'd all be lined up, and everyone'd have to drink worm medicine. And it was orange-flavoured. And because my parents didn't allow pop in the house, it was a treat."

GOING NOWHERE

September 21, 2010

Parliament opened yesterday. Now, in show business, after opening night, that's when you sit back, you take stock, you figure out where we're going to go from here. And looking at this Parliament, thus far, my guess is: nowhere.

None of our political leaders want this Parliament to work. Which is a good thing to know, because that way, when you see them stand up and say they want this Parliament to work, you can judge for yourself how good they are at lying. And speaking of lying, can we please dispel some of the myths that are floating around out there? Can we please stop saying that Michael Ignatieff's Liberal express was a smashing success? Yes, we know, he got on a bus, he went from A to B, he shook some hands, he went to a picnic, he didn't screw up. To hear the Liberals talk about it, you'd swear he should be awarded the Victoria Cross. That's where the bar is for the Liberals right now. He got on a bus all by himself. Most of us did that in kindergarten.

And after this summer, can we please finally stop saying Stephen Harper is a tactical genius? I mean, the guy disappeared for huge periods of time—at one point he went thirty-eight days without being seen in public or answering a single question. I have dead relatives who communicate more than that. And then, when he did come out of the basement, he only did it long enough to abolish the long-form census. Which is genius—if you're running for the leadership of the Flat Earth Society.

So I guess you could say, looking at this Parliament, I'm in a glass-half-empty kind of mood. Right now, I'm just looking for a leader, any leader at all, who will tell the truth, pull the trigger and send us to the polls. Because I don't want an election, I want a whole new cast.

DIVIDE AND CONQUER

September 28, 2010

We've always had big rivalries in this country—always have, always will. French vs. English. East vs. west. Rural vs. urban. Leafs-Habs. Leafs-Sens.

And then, of course, there are your local skirmishes. Heck, you talk to someone from Alberta, you would swear that the rivalry between Calgary and Edmonton is more intense than the one between the Klingons and Starfleet.

Of course, sensible people don't take this stuff too seriously. And I know there are people who do. It is an unfortunate fact of life that, in this country, there are people who like nothing better than to pass judgment on other people based on where they live. And there's a name for those people: idiots. If you think "from Calgary" is an insult, you're an idiot. If you think "from Wadena, Saskatchewan" or "from Ottawa" is an insult, you're an idiot. And if you think "from Toronto" is an insult—well, then, you're John Baird.

The difference being, John Baird is not just another angry little man with an axe to grind. No, he's also one of the most powerful cabinet ministers in the country. And clearly, he's taking his lead from our Prime Minister. Last week, after the long-gun registry vote, we were a country divided. Did the Prime Minister come out and say, "Okay, we've got to figure this thing out. We need to work together. We need compromise on both sides"? No. Instead, he went on the news and said, "The people of the regions of Canada will not stand for this." What does that even mean? Last time I checked, we all lived in a region of Canada.

That's what we are. We are a nation of regions. Why is our Prime Minister, on the news, saying out loud that we will not stand for one another? It's called nation-building, Prime Minister. First you should say it, then you should try it. Because the regions of Canada are not like government employees. You can't just declare war on some of them because you don't like their opinions.

DON'T WORRY ABOUT HARPER

October 5, 2010

It seems to me that the media is a little too obsessed with how controlling Stephen Harper is. I don't really get this debate. I mean, can we blame the Conservatives for wanting this in a leader? A man who is firmly in control? Because Stephen Harper's all that and a bag of chips. And his idea to scrap the long-form census is a perfect example of his abilities.

Scrapping the long-form census has never been an issue among Conservatives. No, this idea, just like rewriting "O Canada," is Stephen Harper's baby. Talk to anyone close to the guy and they will tell you that every now and then, he gets in a funny mood and comes up with his funny ideas.

He just woke up one morning out of the blue and said to his best people, "Hey, what would happen if we scrapped the long-form census and went to a voluntary survey?" And they all said the same thing. "Well, the data will be worthless, scientists will go crazy, business leaders will freak out, and plus, it will cost an extra $30 million."

And Harper said, "Thirty million dollars? I'm sold!" And then he walked into caucus and said, "Hey,

I'm gonna spend $30 million in the middle of a recession getting less-reliable data. Who's with me?" To which 143 Tory MPs started clapping. Again, that is a testament to his abilities. Do you have any idea how hard it is to get 143 seals to do the same thing simultaneously? He's more than a prime minister, he's like Siegfried and Roy all wrapped up in one.

The difference being, of course, that no matter how many tricks he makes them do, none of his MPs will ever make a peep. So let's stop this debate about how controlling Stephen Harper is. We know what he's made of. It's his MPs I worry about.

Rick installs solar panels with Mike Holmes in Oshawa, Ontario.

Mike: "Good job."

Rick: "Now we're cooking with gas. Well, not. Solar. But you know what I mean."

A PROBLEM WORTH RANTING ABOUT

JAMIE HUBLEY'S suicide touched so many people.

Like everyone, I was shocked and dismayed by the news. And then I ranted—of course. Here is that piece again, followed by some reflections on the extraordinary response when it aired.

Let's hope Jamie Hubley's legacy will be that he sparked a national discussion about bullying in schools, and helped to make any kid who feels different feel safer.

MAKE IT BETTER NOW

October 25, 2011

Every year in this country, three hundred kids take their own lives. It is a mind-boggling number. And this past week, one of those kids was Jamie Hubley. He was fifteen, he was depressed and he happened to be gay.

And because this is 2011, we don't just read about a kid like Jamie. We can Google him, and then the next thing you know, you're sitting at home watching his videos on YouTube. And he was gay, all right. He was a great, big goofy gay kid singing Lady Gaga on the Internet. And as an adult, you look at that and you go, You know what? That kid's going places. But for some reason, some kids, they looked at that and they attacked. And now he's gone.

And because this story is all too familiar, we know exactly what's going to happen next. Grief counsellors will go into the school, as they should. But what about the old-fashioned assembly? You know, where the cops show up and there's hell to pay and they find out who's responsible. You know, like when the lunchroom is vandalized. Because the kids who bullied this boy, they know who they are. And more importantly, other kids know who they are.

It's no longer good enough for us to tell kids who are different that it's going to get better. We have to make it better *now.* That's every single one of us. Every teacher, every student, every adult has to step up to the plate.

And that's gay adults, too. Because I know gay cops, soldiers, athletes, cabinet ministers—a lot of us do—but the problem is, adults, we don't need role models. Kids do. So if you're gay and you're in public life, I'm sorry, you don't have to run around with a pride flag and bore the hell out of everyone, but you can't be invisible either.

Not anymore. Three hundred kids is three hundred too many.

ON OCTOBER 15, 2011, Jamie Hubley committed suicide. When I heard the news, I wrote the rant that's reprinted here. It went viral, as they say. Within twenty-four hours, it was being bounced around the world and hundreds of thousands of people were viewing it and sharing it, proving that the issue of gay kids being bullied in schools is tragically universal.

In Australia, it was posted on a popular message board and elicited comments such as "I like this guy's commentary, but if he ever does a second one he should stop walking around in that alley and stand still."

In the United States, it ended up getting tens of thousands of views when it appeared on the popular gay website Qweerty under the headline "Obscure Canadian makes vague but valid point on LGBT suicides."

You can never control what is going to go viral, though there are some unmistakable trends. Until the rant about bullying, my two biggest Internet hits from the show featured baby bears in Algonquin Park and

Mississauga mayor Hazel McCallion in a bowling alley. Cute baby animals and overachieving senior citizens are universally loved.

If, however, I could have chosen one rant to go viral, it would be the one written for Jamie.

This rant was a big departure for me. While not all my rants are funny—as readers of this book can attest—I usually try to be at least mildly amusing. With this rant, there was no such attempt.

When I heard about Jamie's death, I felt like I had been kicked in the stomach. The last thing I wanted to do was write a rant—I wanted to break something. I wanted to punch someone. Fortunately, though, I have very weak arms, the feeling passed, and in the end I ranted.

I don't think that my reaction to Jamie's death was different from most people's. Anyone with a modicum of mental health would find the entire situation tragic and disheartening. The fact that Jamie was gay and I am gay just gave me a different perspective.

Jamie Hubley was out of the closet in high school. That's something I never even contemplated doing when I was in school. Of course, my excuse is that I was a teenager in the olden days. In my day, there was no Internet and there were no gay storylines on TV. We didn't have a gay-straight alliance; all we had was the drama club, which in hindsight is almost the same thing.

But the truth is, I wasn't out in high school because I wasn't as brave as Jamie Hubley. He was the only out kid in his school. I could have been that guy, but I wasn't strong enough. He was a better man than I.

But the fact that a young man as brave as Jamie felt so helpless was a terrible reminder that there is a constituency out there that gay adults need to pay attention to. High school was a long time ago and, like most people, I found that once that building was out of sight, it quickly went out of mind.

And because there were no "out kids" when I was in school, I never really thought about the ones that must be there now, let alone what issues they might face. For my entire adult life, "gay issues" were issues that primarily affected gay adults. Issues such as HIV and AIDS, or equality rights in the workplace. Gay students simply weren't on my radar.

Now, just to be clear: when it comes to whether or not a kid should come out in school, I have no idea what the answer is. Part of me wants to say to a gay kid on the first day of high school, "Look, school is bad enough no matter who or what you are, so put your head down, study hard, move forward, wait for the bell to ring, repeat 672 times, graduate, move to the big city and be a big, happy homo. It will work out, I promise. It gets better." Hardly inspiring words, but that's how my generation did it. Also, this doesn't help the kids who don't have the luxury of choosing when and where they come out of the closet. I'm referring to those fabulous homosexuals who can be spotted at two thousand feet. These kids have the roughest time in school; they are preyed upon by bullies and targeted for being gay before they have figured it out for themselves. Of course, after leaving school, they become much sought after because they are usually brilliant and interesting and fun to be around. Which is little consolation to a budding queen who finds himself in Grade 10 with three more years of public school to look forward to.

Now, I'm not a child psychologist, although I have played one on TV. I don't know what the solution is, though I am sure there are no silver bullets. But I do know from personal experience that for a gay kid, visible gay adults make a difference.

Gays and lesbians are unique minorities because they are usually a minority of one. If you are hassled at school for being Muslim, at least when you go home in the evening, your family is there and they are Muslim too. If you are hassled because you are short, tall, fat, or are even a little, tiny bit different, there generally are other kids in the same boat. Even if you play oboe in school, there's probably another oboe player in the band you can commiserate with, someone you can hang out with and tell each other that it gets better. (For oboe players, sadly, it doesn't really get better.) A gay kid always thinks he or she is the only one.

I know I was convinced I was the only gay kid in my school. Turns out I was wrong; the class of 1989 at Prince of Wales Collegiate has more than its fair share. We just had no way of finding each other. When I found out Bill Parsons was gay, I almost passed out. We were rivals on the same student newspaper. If we knew then what we know about each other now, God knows what trouble we could have caused.

Despite this, I actually had a pretty good time in school. I was never bullied. I dealt with being gay by not dealing with it. Probably not the healthiest choice, but it's the one I went with. I figured I would cross the bridge when I got to it, and for me that meant I would deal with it when I was no longer required to be in a building with eight hundred people every day, a hundred of whom seemed hell-bent on destroying anyone who stood out as different. I also had the added luxury of knowing in my heart of hearts that while my family might be disappointed or upset or confused, they would under no circumstances do anything drastic, like disown me or stop laughing at my jokes.

And while I felt I was alone and I didn't know any gay people personally, there was one very visible gay person I was aware of.

I can remember the moment in Grade 10 when I found out. I was standing on Larkhall Street in St. John's, Newfoundland, when my friend Andrew pointed at a house across from his parents' and said, "Karl Wells lives there. He's married to a dude. They were at Mom's last night for a potluck."

This qualified as stunning news. There wasn't a man, woman or child in Newfoundland and Labrador who didn't know Karl Wells. He was the weatherman on the CBC evening news; but he was much more than just a weatherman, he was a bona fide celebrity—some could say a superstar. He was perhaps the most recognizable face in the province. We take weather seriously in Newfoundland, and it was being delivered by a guy who was married to a dude.

It might seem absurd, but I took great solace in finding out that one of the most liked and respected men in the province was a gay man who lived what appeared to be a very boring, normal life in a bungalow on a suburban street in St. John's.

Andrew was shocked when I looked at him, gazed skyward and announced to nobody in particular, "As God is my witness, someday I too will be a gay weatherman on the CBC!" The rest is history.

That may be an exaggeration, but just a slight one. I never actually told Andrew I was gay that day, and over time I came to realize I was more interested in politics than weather patterns. And anyway, Karl kept that job for another fifteen years.

Decades later, while on a shoot at the RCMP's Depot Division, the Saskatchewan training facility for all RCMP cadets, I had my own reverse Karl Wells moment. A soon-to-be graduate told me that, when he told his mother he was gay, he added "like Rick Mercer." He told me that when he was dealing with his sexuality in high school, he read in *The Globe and Mail* that I was gay and it made a difference to him. Hardly scientific, but it was a nice thing for him to say.

And, yes, for those readers who stopped paying attention after I mentioned a gay soon-to-be RCMP officer, he was very hot, and yes, he was married. Wherever he is now, I know that if there's a young person on his street who's dealing with their sexuality and feeling alone, the fact that there's a six-foot, two-inch RCMP officer down the road "married to a dude" will make a big difference. And if there is a potential bully on the street, he might think twice about calling someone a fag as an insult.

After the rant aired, the response was overwhelming. For a brief period, I became the patron saint of gay teenagers with low self-esteem. It's now on my resumé, along with my ability to type with both hands.

I know that lots of kids get bullied, but hearing from them personally wasn't something I was expecting or was prepared for. And it wasn't just gay kids; so many kids are bullied for so many reasons. Some straight kids get bullied for being gay because it turns out that's a go-to insult used by kids who like to terrorize other kids. I feel particularly bad for these straight kids. They get the lousy parts of being gay, the harassment and the discrimination, without the fabulous stuff, the exotic vacations and free trips, that come later.

And I heard from so many well-adjusted, successful people who wouldn't go back to high school for one day for all the money in the world. And suddenly, people I knew, people I never would have suspected were victims of bullying, told me their horror stories. I thought we were the generation that talked about everything. Apparently not.

And the mothers. Oh God, how many poor mothers did I hear from. When we get to a point where we no longer need an It Gets Better program for the kids, someone has to create an It Gets Better program for the parents.

The media responded to the rant in many different ways, mostly positive. Everyone, it seems, was moved by Jamie's death, and everyone wanted kids to go to school in a safe environment. My suggestion, though, that some gay adults should make themselves more visible rattled a few commentators. *The Globe and Mail* wrote an editorial saying gay adults have no obligation to help gay young people by being visible. They felt this was dangerously close to outing someone against their will. I don't advocate forcing anyone out of the closet. That said, if a famous hockey player can be guilt-tripped out of the closet because it might help some kid in Moncton, then so be it.

In the gay media, the rant was covered, but instead of the message being discussed, it was the messenger. That would be me. I wasn't surprised by this, as the issue of gay kids being bullied had already been covered extensively in the gay media, so the rant was hardly an eye-opener in that community. At least one gay publication ran a piece saying that I was the one not "out enough" and was the last guy who should be telling other gay people to be visible. They might have a point, although the irony is I've been on the cover of the same magazine that suggested it.

I do understand the frustration. There are many gay adults who are much more visible than me. There are activists who have dedicated their life to equality rights for the GLBT community. If it weren't for their work, I wouldn't enjoy the privileges and rights that I do now. For them, it must be slightly galling when TV Boy is moved by the death of a gay kid, mentions it on TV and suddenly it's being bounced all over the Internet.

But I never suggested that all gay adults need to be what we might think of as a traditional "gay activist." I know soldiers who have served in Afghanistan and who are out to all around them. The fact that they are visible to their immediate community in the Canadian Forces sends a message as well. That, too, is activism. Glen Murray is an out gay cabinet minister in Ontario. He's been out for years and has never dodged questions about his sexuality. As a cabinet minister, his job is to dodge questions about government policy. He is very good at it, and that, too, is activism.

Of course, if you happen to be in the public eye, like Glen Murray or certain TV hosts, it's a slightly different dynamic than most civilians face. As I said to Anna Maria Tremonti on CBC Radio's *The Current,* "How many times do you have to come out in this country?"

I had one journalist say, "Well, I've seen you march in the gay pride parade for the past five years, but I had no idea you were out." I was on a float in the gay pride parade with a giant super-soaker. What did he think I was doing there? Hiding? Picking up chicks?

Coming out is a constantly evolving process. By the time I was in my early twenties, there wasn't a single person in my life—my friends, family, neighbours or co-workers—who didn't know I was gay. By normal standards, that is about as out as one can be. That said, I have always had a public life, too, and I never discussed being gay in the media because I felt it was nobody's business. I knew in my heart of hearts that if I was ever asked by a reporter, I would never deny being gay—but, Canada being Canada, nobody really cared and nobody asked and over a decade went by.

It took a while for me to come to the conclusion that this wasn't enough anymore. The average Canadian doesn't care if I am gay, they don't care if a police chief is gay or if a hockey player is gay. I get that. But there are Jamie Hubleys out there, and to them it matters.

It was a personal decision, and honestly one I have never been entirely comfortable with. I'm actually a pretty private person. I've done thousands of radio and television interviews over the last twenty years, I can blather about politics from sun-up to sundown, and the only times I have been thrown for a loop were by a question that was deeply personal. Something along the lines of "What kind of car do you drive?" Or "What's your favourite vacation spot?" Or the dreaded "What are your hobbies?" So the idea that I would go on national television or radio and discuss anything as personal as my sexuality is about as appealing to me as a colonoscopy.

But because these darn kids have gone and decided that they are going to be out of the closet in high school—well, my generation has to do its part to help them out. So I came to the conclusion that, like my annual colonoscopy, it's something that I have to do whether I like it or not. Having done both now for many years, I must say that, thanks to the Valium-Demerol drip, a colonoscopy is infinitely more enjoyable.

——

If anyone in any Canadian workplace randomly punched a co-worker or spit on them or called them "nigger," "fag" or "kike," they would be summarily fired, if not arrested. And yet this type of thing happens every day in Canadian schools—and nobody seems to have a solution. Jamie Hubley's death touched so many people. If he has a legacy, it will be that he sparked a national discussion about bullying in schools.

Jamie tried to start a Rainbow Club in his school—a gay-straight alliance under a different name. He wanted to have a place where kids who felt different for whatever reason could come together, support each other, eat pizza, watch YouTube videos and be like all the other kids.

When he put up the posters for his club, they were torn down by kids who had no tolerance for Jamie, no tolerance for this great, talented kid who happened to be gay. His father tells me he was devastated by that. I can only imagine how thrilled Jamie would be to know that the Rainbow Club now exists in his school and is thriving.

There are similar clubs in many schools across Canada. And hopefully Jamie's legacy will lead to even more, until eventually every school kid in Canada who feels different will have a place they feel safe. And then, hopefully, Jamie's legacy will lead to a day where these clubs are not needed at all.

Flying a Harvard at the Windsor Air Show.

Rick: "What year was the plane built?"

Pilot Edward: "Nineteen forty-one."

Rick: "What year was the parachute packed?"

LETTING DOWN VETERANS

October 12, 2010

I like politics because, in many ways, it is the theatre of the absurd. I love politics for the same reason I love Monty Python. But occasionally, politics can move from the absurd to the obscene just like that. Which brings us to the case of Colonel Pat Stogran.

A Canadian solider, Stogran served his country for thirty years, and then the Tories came along and, with huge fanfare, they gave him a job. A new job—one job and one job only: to stand up for our veterans. A veterans' ombudsman. And boy, do they regret that. Because apparently, he wasn't paying attention when they said, "Oh, and keep your mouth shut." So this summer, when we weren't paying attention, the Tories quietly said it was time for the good colonel to move on.

Why? Well, for starters, he crossed the line when he criticized the veterans' charter. I mean, how dare he? All the parties supported the veterans' charter. Why not—it's a charter! Everyone loves a charter. Everyone loves a veteran. But it was Stogran who said, "No, no, no . . . read the fine print. Under this new charter, disabled soldiers actually get less money than ever before."

So, for all you people who believe this government has never tried to cut costs? Oh, they have—on the backs of injured soldiers. And the only reason we know this is Pat Stogran. So basically, he was fired. And now we find out his personal medical files have been accessed by the government over four hundred times. He's not the only one. If you're a veteran, and you cross the government, your medical files will get passed around like a dirty picture at summer camp.

Pat Stogran deserves the Order of Canada, double the budget and a corner office. Instead, he's being shown the door. He stood up for veterans. Where are the MPs who are going to stand up for *him*?

THE WORLD DOESN'T LIKE US

October 19, 2010

Last week was a tough one for this country. It's not every day that the entire world gets together and says, "We don't like Canada" and we're rejected at the United Nations. Well, in fact, it's never happened before. It's a brand new feeling. So it was very nice of the Tories to provide some comic relief when they blamed Michael Ignatieff.

Now, see, I had no idea the guy was that powerful. But apparently, when the president of the Congo wakes up in the morning, the very first thing he does is turn to page A12 of the *Toronto Star* to see if Michael Ignatieff has been musing.

But all that aside, this crushing humiliation for Canada on the world stage actually had a silver lining for the Tories. It took the spotlight off Jim Flaherty's latest economic update. And in case you missed it, it's very bad news. Canada has now posted the largest yearly deficit in Canadian history. And yes, that includes the years we were fighting the Nazis.

Poor old Jim. He didn't see it coming. Although you would think he'd be used to it by now, because every time he does an economic update, and there have been five, he's wrong. To be fair, he's not always dead wrong; sometimes he's completely wrong. In fact, being wrong is his thing now, it's his trademark. Kind of like Tony Clement's sideburns.

Thank God Jim's just the Minister of Finance; imagine if he did something important, like drive a school bus or work at Tim Hortons. "Hey Jim, I gave you two bucks and asked for a double double. What's up?" "Oh, I'm sorry, sir. Here's an apple juice and twelve dollars change."

Yes, it's been quite a week for Canada. We find out the world doesn't like us and the guy in charge of our money still can't count. Kind of makes you wish you could pretend it never happened—which is exactly what they're hoping for.

REMEMBER TO REMEMBER

November 9, 2010

Canadians are very good at respecting Remembrance Day. If you've ever been lucky enough to attend a ceremony in person, or even watch it live on TV from Ottawa, you know it's not something you'll ever forget. It doesn't get much more moving than that. But for most Canadians, it's a workday, it's a weekday, it's a busy day like any other. It can get away from you.

Last year, I wasn't at a ceremony. I wasn't watching TV. I was squeezing in a haircut. I looked down at my watch, and it was two minutes to eleven. Two minutes to the moment where the entire country chooses to be silent, to reflect on the sacrifice of our war dead. And where am I? I'm wearing a giant bib, there's a woman in one ear telling me she met Rex Murphy in person and he's really quite handsome, there's a guy in my other ear telling me how his appendix exploded. And the music is on full blast. And I ask you: Is this why they died on the beaches?

Well, yes it is, actually. So all of us could go about our busy lives without a care in the world. And so I stepped out on the sidewalk, where it was quiet. And then I came back in and the woman said to me, "Did you go for a cigarette?" And I said, "No—it's November 11, it's eleven o'clock, I wanted a moment of silence." And do you ever have those moments where you just want to take back what you just said? Because as soon as I said it, I felt like the biggest holier-than-thou jerk who ever walked the earth, and she felt worse. Because she didn't mean to forget. It just happened. It can happen to any of us, and we know it shouldn't. So this year let's make sure we remember . . . to remember. By setting your alarm—it's in your phone. And if you don't know how that works, ask your kids. They can show you how your phone works. And you can tell them why we can never forget.

Training with Canada's national rugby team in Langford, B.C.

Rick: "This is not the kind of scrum I'm familiar with. I'm more familiar with 'Mr. Prime Minister! How can Tony Clement still be in cabinet? How many times can you demote him?'"

GILBERT
ZENON
TRAINER BALL

NONE OF OUR BUSINESS

November 16, 2010

Recently, the Prime Minister's Office has been getting a lot of grief over spending. And for no other reason than that the Prime Minister said he was freezing all government departments, and then secretly increased his own budget by 30 percent over two years.

I mean, really, what's the big deal here, people? He's the daddy, and he's saying, "Do as I say, not as I do." And to be fair, this prime minister believes in transparent government. Which is why, as he promised, you can go to his website and see exactly how his office is spending your money. You should do it sometime. And if you can find that link, may I then suggest you turn your attention to finding the exact location of the Franklin Expedition, because clearly you're that good.

When you do find the website, well, I think you'll really enjoy it, especially if you're a fan of fiction. It's all there. Like, you can see what the Prime Minister spent on accommodations for eight nights in Vancouver when he attended the Paralympics: $564—seventy bucks a night. The Travelodge in Sudbury costs twice that much. So either the Prime Minister thinks we're stupid, or they forgot to mention the cost of building the time machine. Because, let's face it, the last person to pay that price for a suite at the Four Seasons died in 1962.

Which may explain a few things, actually. Because, according to his expenses, he also flies all over the world for zero dollars, and consumes no food or beverages. So, in fact, maybe he's beyond transparent; maybe he's a vampire.

Now, personally, I don't care that the Prime Minister spends scads of money. I don't care that he likes suites with pianos. I don't care that he likes to have the whole floor cordoned off to himself. He's the Prime Minister. But being transparent means telling the truth. And when it comes to the Prime Minister's expenses, like everything else in that office, the truth is, apparently, it's none of our business.

KILLED WITHOUT DEBATE

November 23, 2010

I like it when light shines on the Canadian Senate. Because there's no doubt about it, it is a very strange and unique place.

It has been a dumping ground for political hacks and bagmen since Mackenzie King was in short pants. We all know it needs reform. So why is it such a big deal that Tory senators killed a bill? I mean, the Senate has killed bills before, right?

Not really. Not like this. They didn't just kill a bill; they killed a bill without any debate. And that is the entire reason the Senate exists. They are, despite the fact that Mike Duffy is a member, the chamber of sober second thought. And the Tory senators took a bill that had been voted on and passed by a majority of the duly elected members of the House of Commons—the people we actually vote for—and killed it without a debate. To put that in perspective, the last time it happened was the 1930s. Think about this: Jean Chrétien, who we all know would have sold his own mother to get his own way and embarrass the Opposition—he never tried this. It's one of those things that's so undemocratic, nobody actually believed any Canadian government would do it. It's one of those things that's just not done. And so, when Marjory LeBreton, the leader of the government in the Senate, was asked about this, she just laughed and said, "Ha, it's legal." Oh, that's a great defence there, Marjory—it's legal. It's also legal to walk up to a veteran, stick a quarter in his poppy box and take all the poppies. But people don't do it. Because most of us like to think about what's right, not what's legal.

If you're dealing with people who go through life and don't care about right or wrong and don't care about democracy as we know it and only care about what they can get away with . . . all the reform in the world won't make a difference.

With Allan Hawco on the set of Republic of Doyle, *St. John's, Newfoundland.*

Rick: "*Republic of Doyle*—everyone's favourite detective show here on the CBC. And look who it is—the star of *Republic of Doyle*! The 1968 Pontiac GTO."

SCANNERS

November 30, 2010

Well, the holiday season is fast approaching, and this is the time of the year when our thoughts turn to airport security. Because it seems that the media and the federal government are suddenly obsessed with the ethics of the full-body scan and the so-called invasive body search. Which, I believe, is a totally inappropriate term. Let's face it: anyone who has turned forty and had a routine medical exam understands that nothing that happens at the airport should be described as invasive.

It is very simple: if you want to get on a plane, you gotta go through the metal detector, and occasionally, if you're lucky, you get sent to the extra-special touchy-feely line. And when that happens, you go into the body scanner, and then, ten seconds later, you're done.

But yes, it does produce an anonymous, semi-naked image of your body. But do you know whose rights I believe are being violated here? The guy in the basement who has to look at those images for twelve hours a day. I mean, have you ever looked around an airport or a bus terminal in this country? Canadians are a wonderful, proud, lumpy northern people—and we look best with our clothes on. So I don't know what that guy in security did in his past life, but he's paying for it now.

Now, of course, if you don't want the body scan, you can opt for the pat down. And again, I pity the person who does that for a living. I have witnessed rude and aggressive behaviour at airport security more times than I can count. And 99 percent of the time, it is us, the morally outraged travelling public, that are at fault. Look, if you don't like to be touched, take it up with your therapist or your member of Parliament. Because remember, the government makes the rules here, not the folks in the rubber gloves.

So this holiday season, let's say everyone just calm down, remove the coins from our pockets and let security do their job. Because when they do their job, we get home safe.

NEW CABINET

January 11, 2011

Now that the holidays are over and Canadians are back to work, I believe this is a perfect time for all of us to sit back and reflect on all the hard work done by our members of Parliament. No, actually, what I meant to say is it's the perfect time to reflect on the fact that, for members of Parliament, Christmas vacation begins on December 16 and extends all the way to January 31. Kids in kindergarten get less time off at Christmas. But a few of the MPs popped into work last week for the cabinet shuffle. Which was huge news in Ottawa. Because in Ottawa, no matter what happens, it always leads to election speculation. In fact, for some people, predicting there's going to be an election is a full-time job.

Now, of course, the Prime Minister's Office says this is not true, and that the only reason there was a shuffle was because there was a gaping hole in cabinet. Now, personally, I believe that's a terrible way to refer to any cabinet minister—but that is the level of discourse you find in Ottawa these days.

So, how did Harper fill the gaping hole? He inserted Peter Kent. Which sounds more fun than it is.

This is a government that has had five environment ministers in five years. Having the Prime Minister make you the environment minister is a bit like getting a bad result on your CAT scan. And the Prime Minister also made Julian Fantino the new minister in charge of senior citizens. Now, to be fair, Fantino brings a lot of experience to this file. For example, he knows that when dealing with the older folks, you want to dial the taser down a notch or two. And the Prime Minister went out and created a brand new ministry. Making this pretty much the biggest cabinet in Canadian history. There are now more limousines per square foot on Parliament Hill than in downtown Dubai. Which leads me to believe the Prime Minister is preparing to trigger an election. So please, let me join the election speculators and say, in true Ottawa-speak, I believe it is on, it is imminent. I am 100 percent certain, but I could be wrong.

IGGY ON TOUR

January 18, 2011

Canada in the winter. It is a wonderful, stunning, terrible place. But we adapt, we are resilient. Canadians celebrate the winter. In fact, I've done the math: for every twelve Canadians, there are three winter festivals featuring frostbite, tears and hot chocolate for the kids. But there are realities, such as: if you're travelling in this country at this time of year, you can forget about having a schedule. You might as well prepare an itinerary for a voyage through the seventh circle of hell. Sure, your flight is leaving Churchill, Manitoba, at seven-thirty in the morning, but if the ice blowing across the highway is taking the paint off the rental van, there might be some delays. And then you might have to drive. Which can be very dangerous. There is only so much Tim Hortons chili one man can eat. So, that being said, I am thrilled that all of our political leaders have chosen this time of the year to hit the road—because, well, I'm not particularly fond of any of them.

Now, my favourite itinerary belongs to the Michael Ignatieff 20/11 Tour. Twenty towns in eleven days, in the dead of winter. Now, personally, I believe nine towns in eleven days would have been more practical, but I guess "Ignatieff 9/11" doesn't send the right message. So twenty towns it is. Including, tomorrow, Miramichi, New Brunswick. Where two feet of snow is considered a light dusting. He'd better hope that Harper doesn't call a snap election, because a man can go into Miramichi this time of year and be stuck there until the spring. But on the upside, after a couple of weeks snowed in on the floor of a Econo Lodge somewhere, it will be hard to accuse Ignatieff of being out of touch with the average Canadian. So here's to winter, our political leaders and their tight schedules. Wear long johns, embrace the unknown—and easy on the chili.

WHO APPROVED THIS MESSAGE?

January 25, 2011

In politics, attack ads used to be the exception to the rule. And campaign ads outside of a campaign were completely unheard of. And now, both exceptions are the new normal. Canadians are no longer allowed the luxury of sitting down and watching an episode of *Heartland*—a lovely story about a girl and her horse—without being bombarded with a doomsday voice telling us that Michael Ignatieff taught at Harvard. Which, according to the Conservatives, is worse than punching a nun.

Now, don't get me wrong—I don't care if they go after Ignatieff over some policy that he might have. Have at him! I just can't believe, after all these years, they're still harping on about the fact that he worked outside of the country. And I take this personally because I'm from Newfoundland. And like a lot of Newfoundlanders, when I became an adult, I went away to work. In fact, I have worked away from Newfoundland for about as long as Michael Ignatieff worked outside the country. And if Stephen Harper ever looked me in the eyes and said, "You're not a Newfoundlander," I think my head would come off.

Or better yet, I would love to see him say that to, say, Gordon Pinsent, because who doesn't like to sit back and watch an eighty-year-old man slap the hell out of someone half his age.

Negative ads are depressing. I don't care who makes them. And at the end of the day, the entire country suffers because it drags the entire political process right down into the toilet. So if we are going to borrow every horrible political tactic ever developed in the United States, let's take another page from their book. Because at least in the United States, if one party attacks another party, the leader responsible has to pop up at the end and say, "I'm Joe Blow and I approve this message." In Canada, our leaders don't do that. And my guess is they never will. Because that takes courage. And bullies generally have none.

On a date with Danielle Smith, Alberta's Wild Rose Alliance Leader, at the West Edmonton Mall.

Rick: "So, you don't like negative campaigns?"

Danielle: "No."

Rick: "You don't like deficits?"

Danielle: "No."

Rick: "And you don't like caucuses that are gagged?"

Danielle: "That's right."

Rick: "So you're not what you would call a Harper Conservative."

SNOW DAYS

February 8, 2011

Lately, I've taken to listening to talk radio. I go online and I pop around the country and see what people are getting angry about. And boy, we are an angry bunch. Usually, we're angry because someone somewhere is gettin' away with something. But this past week, the anger in this country has been off the charts. And why? Snow days. Parents in Toronto are having full-blown aneurisms. And I have to ask you, what is wrong with the adults in this country? And who are these people calling in and saying that when they were kids there was no such thing as snow days? There were snow days in this country in 1864. The only difference is back then the miserable adults who were complaining couldn't call into a radio station.

Cripes, the kids in Toronto have not had a day off because of snow since 1999. You know what that means? That means there's an entire generation of schoolchildren in Canada's largest city who have no idea what it's like to go to bed at night dreading a math test, only to wake up the next morning and find out, as if by some divine intervention, school has been cancelled. And then they head out, hit the toboggan hill all day, come home, eat supper, pass out because they're exhausted, wake up the next day and botch the math test because they didn't study, because it was a snow day.

And when school is cancelled for no real reason because the big snowstorm doesn't come? Even better. Because when it comes to someone getting away with something for nothing, it doesn't get much better than that. So instead of getting angry about snow days, why don't we celebrate them? Why don't we embrace them for exactly what they are: a rite of passage, a part of being Canadian?

The snow day. It should be put on a stamp.

Ice canoeing in Quebec City.

Rick: "Whose idea was it to put Mike Duffy in the boat?"

MR. HARPER, ARE YOU ON YOUR MEDS?

Maclean's, *April 4, 2011*

Week one of the campaign, and I admit I am starting to side with my friends who occasionally question my sanity for following Canadian politics at all, let alone so closely. "Why in God's name would you pay any attention to that bunch of boobs and losers?" they ask. "Boobs and losers?" I say. "How dare you. These are the best and the brightest that Canada has to offer." Depression kicks in soon after.

Being a political junkie in this country is a bit like being a diehard Leafs fan. Year in and year out, they believe they will witness magnificence and magic, and year in and year out, they witness the opposite. But still they continue to show up, cheer, pay through the nose for a hot dog and leave in tears.

This election certainly started out with a bang. My prediction that the Liberals would, at the last minute, run away and hide behind the dumpsters on Parliament Hill and avoid the vote did not come to pass. The government was defeated on a confidence motion because they were in contempt of the House of Commons. A vote that Stephen Harper immediately claimed did not occur. He didn't deny the semantics of the vote—he simply denied it happened at all, preferring instead to believe his government was defeated on the budget. There is evidence to the contrary—after all, he was there and it was on TV—but still, as far as he is concerned, it didn't happen. Some people might consider this inability to understand or admit to what is happening in one's immediate surroundings symptomatic of a small stroke or a severe concussion, but in Ottawa it's just a symptom of spending too much time around people in the PMO.

I like elections. Governments don't fall every day, but I understand why some people feel that they do. Four elections in two years is a lot. I have baking soda in the fridge that is older than this government, and I still have Tabasco from back in Paul Martin's day.

But elections are important. We all know that $300 million is a lot of money—it is a sobering fact that $300 million could be used to purchase a thousand MRI machines for rural Canada . . . or six gazebos in Tony Clement's riding. But this is a democracy, and this is the cost of doing business.

According to Stephen Harper, this election is about choices. We either elect a stable majority Conservative government or a coalition of liberals, socialists, separatists, criminals and child predators, and not in that particular order.

Michael Ignatieff also says this election is about choice. He says we have a choice between the Red Door and the Blue Door, blissfully unaware that it is not the doors that people are wary of, but the two knobs out front.

Jack Layton says he is the next Prime Minister of Canada. He, too, may be suffering from a concussion.

That said, once the government fell, both Harper and Ignatieff showed that they do things very differently. Stephen Harper made a terse statement on the situation and refused to take questions. Michael Ignatieff made a terse statement on the situation, took questions, but refused to give answers.

How Michael Ignatieff could orchestrate the defeat of the government and launch himself into a campaign without an answer for the coalition question is beyond me. But that was what he did, attempting to dodge the question in both official languages.

At one point, he declared, "I am a democrat," and grabbed his man-breasts in a death clutch. Still, the press was not sated, and he had no other choice but to go home and issue a statement that said unequivocally he would not seek to form a coalition with any other political party.

Over at the Harper campaign, jubilation about the disaster that was Ignatieff's first press conference was short-lived. Turns out Stephen Harper also dabbled with separatist coalitions in the not-so-distant past, and there is proof—not in the form of a forgotten blue dress, but in the form of a letter signed by Harper and Gilles Duceppe and sent to then Governor General Adrienne Clarkson.

Personally, I am shocked that Stephen Harper tried to get in bed with Gilles Duceppe. Experimentation of this kind in college is one thing, but that late in life I think that it probably means you're hiding something that will always be there—namely, a desire to do anything and everything to stay in power.

Jack Layton's post-vote press conference should have gone well. Jack was born for this type of work. Except, instead of talking to Canadians about his version of events, he had to answer personal questions about his health, revealing his prostate-specific antigen numbers. At one point, he offered to remove his clothes right there on Parliament Hill to allow journalists to inspect his scars. Nobody took him up on the offer, Rosemary Barton having not been in attendance.

That said, Jack Layton didn't reveal personal information about his health because the gallery wanted to know; he did it because, earlier that day, Conservatives had fanned out across the country and were practising the dark arts. The whisper campaign they had been conducting about Jack's health was stepped up a notch.

Conservative Senator Mike Duffy, who can perhaps kindly be described as the most amoral partisan hack ever to draw a breath, went on radio in Nova Scotia, a province of potential growth for the NDP, and in the hushed tones usually reserved for a palliative-care unit, told a radio audience that he personally saw Jack on the Hill and "it doesn't look good, Jack doesn't look good . . . he is a valiant man for carrying on."

It takes a certain kind of man to gleefully trade on an opponent's battle with cancer. Mike Duffy is that man. It is why, I suppose, Stephen Harper appointed him to the chamber of sober second thought. I say that if the Conservatives want Jack's prostate to be an issue in the campaign, let all the leaders' health be on the table. Weekly prostate exams for all. And we'd also like to know what meds our leaders are on—or more importantly, what meds they are off—on any given day.

As I write this, the campaign is in full swing. This time around, the Liberals have a plane, chartered from an outfit in Alberta, that looks like everyone else's plane, so nobody is making fun of them. The Conservative plane is chartered from Air Canada, so if you're a journalist, that's the plane to be on. Unlike the Liberal plane, every flight with the Tories gives you Aeroplan travel miles. By the end of the campaign, the journalists will have so many travel miles they will have a card that says "super elite" on it, just like the one John Baird carries.

Harper's plane also has the snazziest paint job. It has the words *Harper* and *Canada* emblazoned on the side, and in an act of humility not seen since the release of James Cameron's *Avatar*, Harper's billing puts his name above Canada's, and in the same size and font. Rumour has it his agent demanded this or he refused to appear. Across the tarmac, it looks like "Harper is Canada," and I suppose that is the point.

We will be seeing these planes a lot over the next five weeks as each leader, with his various campaign workers, minions, sycophants and journalists spread out across the country and visit every province and region, back and forth, multiple times. This is what democracy in action looks like. Because of this never-ending road show, at campaign's end we will have a more informed and engaged electorate—or, at the very least, a bedbug epidemic.

With the bison of Elk Island National Park, Alberta.

Rick: "Bison once roamed this country in the millions, and now they're essentially just in small, isolated, protected pockets. They're like the Liberals."

THEY LIVE FOR CAMPAIGNING

Maclean's, *April 8, 2011*

Michael Ignatieff's campaign is a magnificent triumph! Canadians are seeing a side of the man that they did not know existed, and they are excited about what they see. This is according to the people who work for Mr. Ignatieff and whose future employment prospects are tied directly to his success or failure.

The joy radiating from the Liberal camp in week two reminds me of how my parents reacted when my final Grade 8 report card came in. Eyes darted past the Cs and Bs, the F in gym, past the repetitions of "needs improvement" and past "Still owes sixty dollars to the chocolate almond fund," and finally settled on the most reassuring words any parents could read: "Advance to Grade 9." They could not have been happier. After a year of lowered expectations, it seemed like a miracle. He doesn't have to go to summer school! Clearly, the boy is a genius.

Likewise, the Liberal refrain "Iggy is on fire."

Low expectations are your friend. I learned that lesson in junior high; Ignatieff is just figuring it out now, but it is working for him. So far, he has held his own, hasn't fallen off the podium or wandered down any strange roads pondering in public about "anticipatory hypotheticals." While this is good news for Liberals, low expectations will only take you so far. It may be a good strategy if you are trying to avoid being grounded, but it's a hell of a way to become prime minister.

On the Prime Minister's tour, the word is that the Harper campaign is a disaster! The Prime Minister's photo ops are coming across as stiff and scripted. This is according to people who, I am guessing, haven't watched a Harper campaign before—because this one is no different than his others, and oh, would you look at that—he keeps getting elected prime minister.

Sure, he doesn't look comfortable sitting at a piano, listening to a child serenade him with Lady Gaga's "Born This Way." Can you blame him? Who put that together? "Prime Minister, are you familiar with Ms. Gaga? Good news: turns out she is not a hermaphrodite; that was a wooden phallus she was wearing. Anyway, she has written a gay anthem and this little girl is going to sing it to you. Some of the lyrics are about transsexuals and drag queens, but she might skip those."

And putting the Prime Minister on a four-wheel all-terrain vehicle? He doesn't drive one of those. It's not fair. That's almost as ridiculous as putting him on a stage surrounded by guys doing exercises and having him announce that in five years you might get a tax cut if you join a gym, golf club or bathhouse. Oh wait, he did that too.

Personally, I would ditch these awkward staged moments. Harper's happy place is on stage, talking to the party faithful about all the horrible things that will befall the nation if he is not elected. There he shines, and there he connects with Canadians who are sitting at home watching TV and, I guess, being afraid. Ignatieff, on the other hand, is standing on his stage, but has yet to connect. The polls reflect that.

But these men, Iggy and Harper, are the superstars. They are used to seeing their pictures in the newspaper. They are used to the highs and lows of being on the national stage. But there are many races happening in this country, and for those who toil in the back benches, this is their moment.

It's not very often that you find all members of Parliament and all candidates in agreement, but they agree on this. They view the job of MP as a great public service, and they like to remind us it is a noble one. They also agree that campaigns are a tough slog, but it is a sacrifice they are willing to make.

It's the relatives and friends of politicians I feel bad for, because God forbid you are related to one, or friends with one, or happened to go to school with one, or even made eye contact with one. They are a needy bunch. It's like having a drug addict in the family. They want money from you constantly. And on top of that, they demand your time and energy.

A politician's hand is always out, especially during, before and after a campaign, and also before the next one.

Imagine if, in order to keep your job, every so often you had to call everyone in your family, every friend, your in-laws, everyone in your yearbook, and say, "I'm reapplying for my job again. Can I have five hundred dollars? Also, can you take time out of your busy schedule to show up at some long-forgotten Knights of Columbus hall and chant my name over and over again? And when I speak, can you cheer like you are witnessing Martin Luther King recite 'I have a dream,' even though we both know I don't have a clue?"

Most of us go through life trying to avoid hitting up our friends and family for money, and sure, while there are times when it may be inevitable, we try to avoid it becoming a habit. Politicians are that rare breed. This doesn't bother them. They are missing the dignity chip. A career politician like John Baird has, in his lifetime, asked more strangers for more money than all the squeegee kids in Canada combined. This is a sacrifice he and so many others are willing to make.

So what is it that allows these men and women to swallow their pride and say, "Yes, I will do this, I will stand for public office"? I do not know.

Everywhere they go, they have to stare at billboards and posters with their faces emblazoned across them as if they were suddenly transformed into Hollywood stars. They have to do media—sometimes many interviews a day. Which, for an MP used to begging to get on local radio, can be exhausting. And then there is the constant barrage of volunteers to be managed, the old and experienced hands who do the heavy lifting mixed in with the young and impressionable keeners—the ones who wear tight T-shirts with your name across the front who never get tired of listening. And yes, there is the chanting and the applause.

Politicians may very well believe in public service, but for the vast majority it is the campaigns they live and die for; it is why they are on put on earth.

It is why, when you hear Stephen Harper saying he wishes there wasn't an election, that's like a dog saying he has grown tired of licking himself. It's not true—not now, not ever.

Following Fashion Week with Jeanne Beker in Toronto.

Rick: "What can we expect?"

Jeanne: "We can expect a celebration of Canadian fashion, of course. This is a week-long shot at putting great Canadian style on the runway, and everyone's very happy and proudly waving the flag because it's all about Canada. Are you wearing Canadian?"

Rick: "Yes. Stanfield underwear."

A NEW CANADIAN PERSPECTIVE

Maclean's, *April 15, 2011*

My friend Farid is from Iran. This will be the first federal election in which he is eligible to vote.

Being somewhat of a sap, and knowing what a hard-working new Canadian he is, I was immediately moved by this notion. Surely, after a lifetime of persecution in Iran, after making his way to Canada with nothing, after receiving his Canadian citizenship, he would be overwhelmed with joy and excitement at the notion of exercising his democratic right to a vote.

No dice. He is entirely underwhelmed by his choices. "Rick, if it was a choice between PC or Mac, *that* I could understand; but this election, it seems the choice is one lousy PC and another lousy PC—why does it matter?"

Assuming the lousy PCs he was referring to were Michael Ignatieff and Stephen Harper, I suggested that he should look at the NDP. "It was the NDP," I said, "that gave us universal health care. They are passionate supporters of the working man and they fight for the little guy. Jack Layton is a good man," I told him. "He walks the walk and talks the talk. He has solar panels on his barbecue." I could tell by the look on Farid's face that suggesting he vote NDP was akin to insulting his mother, his wife, or both.

I shouldn't be surprised at Farid's dislike of the NDP. While he did flee Iran with his life, he has an affinity for a stern hand on the tiller. During the municipal election in Toronto, Farid became a big supporter of now-mayor Rob Ford after Ford offered the opinion that there were too many people in Toronto and we shouldn't welcome more. Farid's pet peeve is road congestion, so he too would like to see a stop to anyone else moving into the city, especially from other countries.

Being a civic-minded Canadian, I informed Farid that Rob Ford could say whatever he wanted, but that freedom of movement was a fundamental Canadian right and that no mayor, no prime minister, no police officer, no person could tell any citizen or landed immigrant where they can and cannot live.

"Fine," said Farid, "then pass a law saying any new Canadian moving to Toronto should not be allowed to own a car." Irony is lost on the man.

I find my little chats with Farid distressing, but I wanted him to understand fully the importance of voting, and I wanted him to know that there are many other options available to Canadians. Sure, these other parties are less mainstream than the Liberals, Conservatives and NDP, but they are political parties all the same. One million people voted for the Green Party in the last election, and say what you want, that is exciting. And it wasn't long ago that a handsome young Preston Manning announced the formation of the Reform Party and changed the political course of Canada forever. Farid was dubious, and so I logged on to the Elections Canada website to prove it.

In the last general election, there were a baker's dozen of "fringe parties," and their websites prove democracy is alive and well in this country. I learned a lot.

Did you know that Canada has not one, but two national communist parties? There is the Marxist-Leninist Party of Canada and the Communist Party of Canada. This is important to know in case you plan on sending a cheque to one and you get them mixed up. It's a terrible feeling knowing you have put your hard-earned dollars towards the wrong communists.

Both have long histories in this country. In fact, the Communist Party slogan is "Celebrating ninety years." Our current governing party has only been around for seven.

The Marxist-Leninist Party of Canada is somewhat of an offshoot of the original Communist Party; its leader had a falling out with the other, original group when China and the Soviet Union began squabbling in the seventies. They both took separate sides, and a divide took hold among Canadian communists that to

this day is not healed. They are comrades no more.
And like the Canadian Alliance and the Progressive Conservative Party of Canada of old, they continue to run candidates and split the communist vote, making their dreams of forming a majority government even more elusive. At present, both parties deny there are any ongoing merger talks.

Farid was fascinated to learn that the Bloc Québécois is not the only separatist party in Canada. Yes Farid, western Canada has xenophobes as well.

The Western Block Party is lead by Doug Christie, the same Doug Christie who has made a name for himself defending the rights of wannabe Nazis to be, well, wannabe Nazis. These days, Doug has other priorities—namely, seeing western Canada split and form its own country, and, of course, lower taxes. A visit to his website indicates that the first act of an independent western-block nation would be to stop spending money on sewage treatment plants because, and this is a quote from the party platform, "Nature already provides us with an effective, inexpensive and environmentally beneficial treatment system."

It's enough to give separatists a bad name; after all, the Bloc Québécois wants Quebec to separate, but they have never suggested an added benefit of sovereignty would be the ability to turn *la belle province* into a massive toilet.

Thankfully, Farid is an engineer by trade and was baffled as to why anyone would be against sewage treatment.

Personally, my favourite new party on the Canadian political spectrum is also the one with the snazziest website and best name: the People's Political Power Party of Canada, which I'm guessing is not affiliated with anyone with a speech impediment.

Its platform is laid out in a very sophisticated website, and I would suggest that the founder and leader of the party, Roger Poisson, has perhaps the most honest and intriguing biography of any political leader I have read. It reads, in part, "For the last seventeen years, Roger has been working for no wages. He holds no bank account in his name and has no savings. He was learning how to father a nation." I'd like to see Michael Ignatieff or Stephen Harper say that.

Mr. Poisson's platform is extensive, but it does not appear to be fully costed. Unfortunately for the Peoples Political Power Party of Canada, that is a deal-breaker for Farid.

The link to the Marijuana Party of Canada at Elections Canada doesn't work. I'm sure somewhere there is a well-intentioned young man who means to get around to fixing it, but with days to go until the general election, really, what is the rush?

When you track down the website, it turns out to

be nothing but a number of sponsored links to indoor hydroponic growing kits, natural lawn care companies and the NDP. So I can't really say what the Marijuana Party stands for, but I informed Farid that it was a safe bet that they are against the Harper plan of mandatory federal jail time for anyone caught with six marijuana plants growing among the tomatoes.

For those Canadians interested in these parties, there is a debate of the "fringe parties" scheduled to be held in Toronto on April 23. As I write this, it is not clear which parties will show up. One thing we know for certain is that Elizabeth May, after being shut out of the main political debate, has refused to attend. According to her, the Green Party is a mainstream movement and has no place at the fringe table.

As a result, Ms. May has announced plans to debate herself at some later date. I would suggest the first question she might ask is why she continues to run against cabinet ministers.

The leader of the Marijuana Party has agreed to attend, but only if someone pays for his ticket from Vancouver. I approached the publisher of this magazine, suggesting they pay his airfare, but they declined, citing the Marijuana Party's position on corporate income tax reductions.

At the end of this exercise, Farid was more confused than ever but amazed that Canada allows such parties to exist. Again, the concept of total freedom is one we take for granted. There is a bit of a learning curve when you spend all of your life in a country like Iran.

So, when pushed, Farid decided that he was—like so many Canadians—an "undecided" voter. He would make his final decision on election day.

He admits that he likes Ignatieff and agrees he is a very smart man. "But," said Farid, "he didn't come back for me." I didn't bother saying, "How the hell could he? You just got here yourself."

But my guess, if I were a magic vote compass, is that he is leaning towards the Conservatives, despite what he calls a lacklustre campaign. In fact, the only thing Stephen Harper has done to impress him thus far was having the RCMP pull the little girl from his rally because of her Facebook picture with Michael Ignatieff. "Why the big fuss?" he said with a smile. "That reminds me of home."

Like that was a good thing.

Shooting the rapids on the Kananaskis River, Alberta.

Rick: "And this rapid that we're looking at here . . . what's that one called?"

Guide: "This is called the Widow Maker."

Rick: "The Widow Maker! I love a body of water with a nickname. Can we start with one called Gail?"

THIS CHANGES EVERYTHING

Maclean's, *May 9, 2011*

Having led the Conservative Party to a majority government, with the Liberal Party lying bloodied and dying at his feet, Stephen Harper saw the breadth of his domain and wept, for he had no more worlds to conquer.

Twenty-four hours before Canada went to the polls, I went on BBC Radio International to explain to a very pleasant radio personality with excellent diction why Canada was having yet another election.

Now, it's one thing to go on the radio and blather about politics in Canada—the audience knows the cast of characters and it's safe to assume they are somewhat familiar with our recent history. But when you go on BBC International, the audience is in the tens of millions worldwide and you have to bear in mind that the average listener is likely tuning in from a shantytown in Nigeria or a loft in Oslo.

How do you explain in a few minutes just what an accomplishment a majority would be for the Conservative Party? How do you explain how

Stephen Harper became the leader of a grassroots western-based regional party, a party that existed solely to give voice to individual MPs, and somehow transformed it into a national party so centralized in its power structure that no more than five of its MPs are allowed to speak in public?

And how in God's name do you explain that the demise of the Liberal Party would be a seismic shift on our political landscape? And really, did anyone have an explanation for the orange crush?

And why, my Nigerian friends may wonder, did the last-minute revelations of a visit to a sketchy massage parlour fifteen years ago lead to increased support for the leader of Canada's socialists, especially among separatists in Quebec?

How do you explain that Michael Ignatieff was shaping up to be a loser of Ben Johnsonian proportions, not for having cheated or for having lied, but for having been vilified for doing too many things in his life and for having lived in too many places?

Yes, my Nigerian brother, in Canada, time spent at the Velvet Touch massage parlour is a positive; time spent at Harvard, not so much.

And speaking of Quebec, why, on the eve of the election, was the most senior government cabinet minister in that province, the Minister of Foreign Affairs, facing certain defeat at the hands of a part-time karate instructor, a collector of medieval weapons and one-time member of the Communist Party?

One assumes the phone lines at Immigration Canada did not light up that night.

Luckily, the conversation soon turned to something any person with a passing knowledge of democracy could understand no matter where they lived: election night. It was shaping up to be a barn burner, and the host assumed—correctly—I would be glued to the results. "But," she inquired, "is the rumour true that Twittering about election results in Canada as they come in is a criminal offence?"

Yes, I was loath to admit, Elections Canada was attempting to succeed where Hosni Mubarak in Egypt and Mahmoud Ahmadinejad in Iran had failed. They were attempting to stop people from tweeting.

When the interview was over, off the air, I declined an offer to be interviewed the following night after midnight to report how it all turned out. This was a wise stroke of foresight. I know me. Why is that man yelling and why is there the sound of ice clinking in a glass?

The producer of the program wasn't too disappointed. Canadian election results hardly warrant great international scrutiny, especially in the aftermath of Osama bin Laden's death and sexy Will-and-Kate honeymoon updates.

By now, we all know that on election night it was all over by 10:15 Eastern, with most networks declaring a Conservative majority.

For many Conservative voters, this was simply closing the deal on Stephen Harper's promise of a stable government for the next four years; it was a vote for more of the same, please. For others, this indicates that Canada has finally taken a big step to the right, and they hope to see a very different Canada emerge.

All we do know right now is that the animal farm in Ottawa has changed dramatically. The formerly cocky and entitled Liberal, an animal that once roamed wild in the nation's capital, has ceased to exist. In its place, we have a population explosion of a new breed of NDPer. Not only have their numbers doubled, but they have gone from earnest to unctuous in one historic night. Very soon, they will gather in Stornaway—Jack will play guitar, they will shake their lentil jars and plot the next once-impossible step. They have supplanted the natural governing party of Canada in opposition; next stop, 24 Sussex Drive. God give me the strength to sit through any of those conversations.

And then there are the Conservatives: the staffers, the supporters, the MPs themselves. For them, a majority is uncharted territory. This changes everything.

Liberals, even when in opposition, are always surprised when they meet someone who isn't a Liberal. They tend to believe everyone looks at the world the way they do.

Conservatives are the opposite. No matter how much success they achieve, they constantly believe someone is out to get them. Conservatives always believe they are swimming against the current, even when there is ample evidence to prove otherwise. This has served them well; it has allowed them to remain united and focused. The one ideological characteristic all Conservatives in Ottawa share is a complete loyalty to the authority of Stephen Harper and his quest for a majority. But along the way, a lot of Conservatives have been told to sit down and shut up and wait for the big day. Now that it's here, what now?

Will the Prime Minister take this opportunity to relax, be more amicable, comfortable in the knowledge that the Opposition's power has been erased? I think we all know the answer to that. Or will Mr. Harper go to work and salt the earth, and remove the subsidies to political parties, making it more difficult for the Opposition to function? And more importantly, will he be able to keep his own troops down on the farm now that they have seen the glory that is a majority?

All we can be certain of is that, for the time being, with a comfortable majority in the House, Stephen

Harper will do whatever the hell he wants. That's what Canada voted for.

The more pressing question is, What will the Liberals do? The talk on election night, despite Harper's historic victory, was all about them. In four years from now, on election night, will the Liberals be mentioned at all?

Some people, Liberals among them, say this is the best thing that could happen to the party. It's been called tough medicine, the political equivalent of a bankruptcy protection that will force them to restructure and refocus. But this is not just a train wreck for the Liberal Party. This is Lockerbie. Yes, this is a plane crashing into a Scottish village. If you are a Liberal, it must be very hard to imagine any good coming out of this.

But election results are not random events; they are not natural or manmade disasters; they are just that—results.

And the results are stunning. A Conservative majority, the rise of the NDP, the annihilation of the Bloc Québécois, the near death of the Liberals. We saw two national leaders get defeated and Elizabeth May win. In Quebec, a nineteen-year-old voted in his first federal election, for himself, and is now a newly elected NDP MP. Had he lost, he would have sought summer employment at a golf course.

We have had forty-one federal elections in this country, and one hopes the plan is to have many more. And if history has taught us anything, it is this: we show up at the polls and, at the end of the night, governments may rise and governments may fall. For some of those running, it will be the greatest night of their lives; others will find themselves in the glare of TV lights, wearing a smile while secretly cursing the day they considered public service.

And while we ponder the results and study what happened, and speculate about what it all might mean for Canada, it doesn't hurt to think about what didn't happen on election day. No shots were fired, no cars were burnt, nobody was intimidated at the polling booth and nobody died.

And while that mightn't make headlines on the BBC World Service, that's exactly the way it should be. It's why we are a nation worth voting for.

At the Vancouver Circus School with author Ryan Knighton.

Rick: "For those of you who don't know your story: you went blind but didn't notice."

Ryan: "Yes, I lost my sight very slowly."

Rick: "It snuck up on you. And you had lots of car accidents."

Ryan: "I did. I had twelve."

Rick: "How did you get your licence? That's a little embarrassing for the guy who passed you. Did they do this on the test?" *(Waves hand in front of Ryan's face.)*

Ryan: "Did they do what?"

Rick: "Exactly."

THE URGE TO MERGE

September 13, 2011

Well, what a difference a summer makes. Who could have guessed a few months ago that, just like that, both opposition parties would have interim leaders? What does it mean? Does anyone care? And should these parties seize on this historic moment and merge, creating one centre-left party?

Now, this is a very emotional debate if you're a political activist. And don't get me wrong—there's nothing wrong with political activists. They're important people to all parties. These are the people who work the phones and put the signs on the lawn. These are the people who have dedicated their lives to creating a political climate in this country that most Canadians feel is vile and disgusting. They do good work. So, for argument's sake, let's just remove them from the equation. Which is actually very easy.

Less than 2 percent of Canadians belong to a political party, and very few of them actually work on the campaigns. When it comes to this merger business, the average voter is far more practical. If someone voted Liberal or NDP in the last few elections, they don't care about some bad blood left over from some hard-fought battle in upper, inner, outer, lower. No, they're just mad that the Tory keeps getting elected.

So my advice to both parties: unless you love the aroma of opposition, it's shotgun wedding time. Take Jean Chrétien and Ed Broadbent, put them in a room with a pen and paper, a six-pack of beer, put the Barry Manilow on the turntable, lock the door and let the magic happen. And don't let them out until they've got an agreement. Don't worry, they're both old. They'll want to be in bed by ten.

Do that, and the entire thing could be settled by this time tomorrow. The activists will say, "What just happened?" The voters will say, "What took you so long?"

CANADA KILLS

September 20, 2011

It must be terrible to find out that someone you love is guilty of a serious crime. Imagine if you found out that, when you weren't looking, they were busy killing people.

It would be like finding out that while you were enjoying your summer vacation, your country, a country you love unconditionally, Canada, stood virtually alone on the world stage against one hundred other countries and stopped asbestos from being declared a hazardous material. I mean, we all know it's hazardous. If you breathe it, you will die. It's not a question of if, but when. It's as simple as that.

Which is why, when it's used in Canada, if you want to go within ten thousand feet of the stuff, you are required to have a respirator, a hazmat suit and a string of rosary beads. Not that we use it very much anymore. The whole "it will kill you" thing has really affected sales. So instead, we mine it and we ship it to the Third World. And because of us, because of Canada, it's not labelled as hazardous. There is footage of workers in India unloading Canadian asbestos by hand; the stuff is floating in the air like the aftermath of a sorority pillow fight. Women in India are hired to weave Canadian asbestos into fabric.

Meanwhile, here in Canada, we're spending tens of millions of dollars removing all asbestos from the Parliament Buildings and the Prime Minister's residence. Which we should. But the fact that we're spending millions more ensuring that we can sell it to the Third World without warning them puts us in criminal territory.

Prime Minister, the Maple Leaf is a great brand. It stands the world over for the true north strong and free. Let's not put "killer" on the list.

A LESSON IN IRONY

September 27, 2011

Stephen Harper likes to remind us that he got elected by promising to cut government spending. And boy, is he serious about it. How serious? He's gone out and hired some guys from Bay Street in Toronto to tell him how to do it. And what a bargain. The Harper government is paying these guys ninety thousand dollars a day for eight months. It works out to be about twenty million dollars.

Now, there are a few ways you could look at this. Some people may say this is an egregious waste of taxpayers' money, but not me. But then, I'm a glass-half-full kind of guy. I prefer to look at this as a teaching moment. You know, for the kids. The concept of irony is introduced in Canadian schools at about Grade 8, and many teachers say it is a difficult one for the children to grasp. Not anymore, thanks to Mr. Harper. The idea of spending ninety thousand dollars a day to get tips on how not to spend money—that is the new textbook definition of irony. A five-year-old will understand irony after this.

I understand that sometimes you have to pay the big bucks for an expert. Last month, I hired a plumber to fix my toilet, because I don't know how to do that. The difference is, I didn't run around the country telling everyone that I was the only guy in Canada who could fix the toilet, which is what Harper did. And now he's had to go out and hire these consultants who have no experience balancing this country's books to tell him how to do it.

Hey Steve, I've got an idea. Why don't you give Paul Martin a call? He's got experience. I mean, I know he was pretty loopy when it came to being prime minister, but as a finance minister, he knocked it out of the park. Or better yet, why don't you call the last Conservative finance minister who left the country's books in better shape than when he found them?

Oh, right. That would be Sir Samuel Tilley, who died in 1896.

Come on, Steve, save us all twenty million—give Paul a call.

At the 35th annual Canadian Finals Rodeo, Edmonton.

Rick: "There's a lot of prize money up for grabs: $1.27 million! You know what the richest literary prize is in Canada? Fifty grand, for the Giller."

KEEP CALM AND CARRY ON

October 4, 2011

I am not by nature a nervous person. I'm not brave, I'm just not nervous. Because, luckily, I've learned to ignore everything politicians have to say.

This is a good thing, because in Canada, every time you turn around, another Harper cabinet minister is in a full-blown panic. It's like they believe their number-one job description is to freak Canadians out. It's at the point now where if Vic Toews or Jason Kenney ran into my house in the middle of the night screaming "Fire," I'm not moving until I smell smoke.

It doesn't matter what the issue, the message is always the same: be afraid, Canada, be very afraid. And build more prisons.

And the Prime Minister? The only time he seems happy is when he's hanging out with Nickelback, or he's leaning forward, reminding us once again that we live in perilous times, that danger is lapping at our shores. Winston Churchill was more upbeat at the height of the Blitz.

Meanwhile, statistically, we are living in the safest time in our entire history. Crime is down. You would think the government might remind us of that on occasion. I mean, it's a good-news story. Crime is down. But instead, they say, "Well, crime is down, but unreported crime is up." Who does that? That's like instead of telling your kid there's no monster under the bed, you say, "Well, there are no *reports* of monsters under your bed. But unreported monsters? Who's to say?"

Why would a government want people to be afraid? Because people who are afraid, they do what they're told. They pass over their lunch money. They keep their mouths shut.

Don't fall for it. There's nothing to fear but fear itself, and the people who benefit from spreading it.

ON THE FENCE

October 11, 2011

I admit I don't spend that much time thinking about border security. Most Canadians don't. Which, I guess, is something we should be thankful for. But then again, Canadians and Americans have always had different views about this sort of thing. Canadians are taught in Grade 6 that Canada and the United States share the world's longest undefended border, and we think that's cool. Whereas most Americans don't learn about the undefended border until after they're elected to Congress—and then they panic.

Which brings us to the brand new Canada–U.S. border security agreement, which we need for obvious reasons. The problem is that the Americans say it's a done deal, whereas our government will neither confirm nor deny. Now, luckily, the Americans have this crazy idea that people who are affected by this kind of thing have to be consulted. So while our side is saying nothing, we know that the U.S. Border Protection agency has asked every border state across the continent how they feel about a giant fence being built along the 49th parallel.

Sheesh, was it something we said?

But then again, if the guy next door wants to build a fence, there's really not much you can do about it, other than to say, "Hey, we don't want the ugly side facing us, okay? No bolts and uprights and stuff, and, uh, you gotta paint both sides. And, uh, how about you lay off the pressure-treated latticework?"

It's a very slippery slope. Next thing you know, we're standing there in our housecoats yelling, "Hey, any tennis balls come over here, we keep."

Hopefully, it won't get to that. And hopefully, before our government signs any agreements about our privacy, our security or the border, we get a peek at the fine print.

BIGGER ISN'T ALWAYS BETTER

November 1, 2011

It's not every day that government gets it right. But sometimes they do. Our Prime Minister has been consistent in his promise to create smaller government. And he has delivered.

I mean, yes, sure, he is tied with Brian Mulroney for having the largest cabinet in Canadian history, at thirty-nine ministers. And yes, some simpler countries, like the United States, they get by with twenty-three cabinet ministers. But to be fair, a lot of our cabinet ministers are not that bright. If they didn't have this job, they might have to turn to crime or public broadcasting. And this government is tough on both.

But as the old adage goes, sometimes you have to spend money to make money. Which is why, in an effort to make government smaller, Stephen Harper is making it bigger by creating thirty new members of Parliament. Who among us, when contemplating the major problems of the day—poverty, unemployment, Tony Clement—has not said, "If only we had more members of Parliament, everything would be okay"? Suddenly, I don't feel bad that the people who take the search-and-rescue calls from drowning fishermen are being laid off because we're getting new MPs.

See? It's all about balance.

Now, don't get me wrong—I'm all for electoral reform. Many geeks with an obscure interest in the subject are. But before we add new MPs, why don't we fix some of the problems with the existing MPs? Like the fact that we are the only parliamentary democracy in the entire world where an MP does not have the right to stand up and ask a question not approved by their leader. Yes, freedom of speech is a right we all enjoy in this country, unless you're a member of Parliament. And a bill addressing this very problem was killed last year in committee.

So really, if Stephen Harper's idea of job creation is creating thirty new MPs, why don't we save ourselves a pile of cash? Get thirty old mannequins, throw them up in the back row of the House of Commons, sit back and see if anyone notices.

Boxing with George Chuvalo in Toronto.

Rick: "I need a tip! I need a tip!"

George: "You know what I would suggest? You take off your gloves and leave the ring."

HEADS UP

November 8, 2011

I love Canada in November. It's that magical time of year when so many of us get up and go to work, and it's dark. And then we come home from work, and it's dark. They say it leads to Seasonal Affective Disorder. Canada: the birthplace of SAD.

But I've got to say, on my way to work this morning I wasn't so much concerned about the lack of sunshine and my mood as I was with the two pedestrians I almost ran over. And believe me, the fact that it was just two of them means this was a good day.

Why did I almost run them over? Well, as I mentioned, it was dark—a fact that seems to be lost on the vast majority of pedestrians this time of year. That, and I swear to God one of them was dressed head to toe in black. Might as well have been wearing a burka or a cloak of invisibility. If it weren't for the tiny light coming from the cellphone he was texting on in the middle of the street, I would have hit him at forty kilometres an hour.

And is it just me, or do pedestrians in this country actually slow down when they have to cross the street? I believe they do. Science will back me up on this.

Now, don't get me wrong—I've been a bad pedestrian. I know that we all have. Just last month, I was texting with my sister, and was halfway through the crosswalk when it dawned on me: *I'm in the middle of a busy street, my head is down and I'm texting. If I die in the next five seconds, it's my own fault. And not only that, but the people I know, the people who love me the most, they will make fun of me, at my funeral, probably via text.*

Now, I don't know what the solution is here. I'm not a nanny-state guy. I'm not saying everyone's got to slap on a safety vest when they go to work in the morning. But the average person weighs 150 pounds. A Prius weighs 3,000 pounds, and it's dark out. Do the math.

So heads up, Canada. Let's get through this winter together. Better SAD than sorry.

TIME TO CLOSE THE COMMONS

November 29, 2011

Conservative member of Parliament Rob Anders fell asleep last week, live on national television, right in the middle of Question Period. It was on the news a lot, and people found it funny. Meanwhile, in Toronto last year, some dude whose job it was to sell subway tickets took a nap on the job and it was front-page news. People acted like he was history's cruellest monster. It was very telling.

As time marches on, society changes; and with it, traditions die. It's tough, but someone has to say we're closing down the buggy-whip factory, or, that's it, the VCR is going in the garbage. No one wants to be the one to stand up and say the emperor has no clothes, so let me. It's time to close the House of Commons—permanently. Let's face it, it's a soap opera, its ratings are in the toilet and, like all soap operas, it's filled with bad actors and nobody knows their names.

The first job of any MP is to hold government accountable for spending our money. They don't do that anymore. MPs approved fifty million dollars for border security. The Prime Minister took the money and built a hockey rink and a gazebo in Muskoka.

And nobody cares! Which is fine. The second job of an MP is to debate bills in Parliament. Those days are over. An agriculture bill in Cuba gets more debate than a Canadian crime bill. And nobody cares, which is fine.

But if MPs aren't going to do their jobs and they can't keep their eyes open long enough to pretend they're doing their jobs, why send them to Ottawa? Keep them in their ridings. Let them do something useful, like help someone fill out a passport application.

And for the rest of the country, can we finally acknowledge what everyone in Ottawa knows but no one will say out loud: MPs and cabinet ministers have nothing to do with running this country. This country is run by twenty-three-year-olds who work in the Prime Minister's Office. They decide what bills are passed; they decide what countries we invade. Let them do their job.

And the Prime Minister? Well, he can be CEO or Sun God or whatever he wants to be called. He can wear a gold hat. As long as he comes out on a balcony occasionally, waves, goes back in, does his thing, comes out five years later and stands for re-election. But it's his show and his show only. Let's stop pretending it's anything else but. And on that point—there is no debate.

ON LIBERTY AND BALLS

December 6, 2011

I don't know what's sadder—that this country woke up a few weeks ago and read the story about a school in Toronto banning the use of soccer balls on the playground, or the fact that deep down, none of us was really surprised.

I know I wasn't, because I am familiar with the Vice-Principal Law of Enjoyment, which states that for every instance of a child having fun, there is an equal or slightly more powerful force that exists solely to stop that activity from happening.

And every generation is different. When I was in Grade 8, my school banned the Rubik's Cube. Why? Because some kid was wandering down the hall with his head buried in the Rubik's Cube, went headfirst into a door and split his nose open. And I'm sorry, I remember that kid—he was always walking into doors. In fact, if I bumped into him today, I wouldn't recognize him without the nosebleed.

But the school's rationale was, "Well, we can't have kids walking around with their heads down," so they banned the cube. Meanwhile, it is because we wandered around with our heads buried in our Rubik's

Cubes that my generation can safely navigate through traffic on foot with our heads down while texting on our BlackBerries. You could say it saved our lives.

This is a war on fun. And it is a slippery slope. In 2014—and this is a fact—school clubs in Ontario will no longer be able to fundraise by selling chocolate. Only nutritious items. There's your future, Canada: a sad child on your doorstep, trying to sell you a bag of radishes so they can go on a band trip.

Get used to it. Because if you let them take your balls, your freedom is the next to go.

PRIME MINISTER DAD

January 17, 2012

Democracy is very messy. In fact, on paper, it doesn't even make a heck of a lot of sense. For starters, it involves all of us—and by all of us, I mean the people. And what's worse, that means it involves people's opinions, a situation that only leads to debate. And let's face it, no matter what the issue, for every sensible person on either side, there are two idiots who are addicted to the sound of their own voice. I should know: I'm one of them.

But speaking of debate, I've noticed lately that some of the messy parts of democracy are slowly being done away with. Remember debate? No, neither do I. It's been a while.

For example, a couple of months ago, Stephen Harper decided to change the name of the Canadian Navy to the Royal Canadian Navy. There was no debate. He just announced it. Now, personally, I don't care one way or the other, but people in the navy do. Some of them love it, some of them hate it. But the important thing is, nobody asked for their opinion. Who cares what they think? They just serve in the

navy. Who cares what *we* think? We just pay for it.
Nope, Dad said, end of story.

And now we have this pipeline business. Now, I realize I should have paid more attention to this a year ago, but like a lot of Canadians, I find it's only showing up on my radar now. And honestly, I don't know if the pipeline is a good idea or a bad idea. But the good news is, I no longer have to look at both sides. None of us does. No, because Dad has made it perfectly clear, there's only one side to this issue.

And anyone who thinks otherwise is an enemy to Canada. I've got to say, this is way better than the old days, when we had the burden of being informed citizens on our shoulders. No, now we have a new job: to be seen and not heard. Welcome to Canada 2012. His house, his rules. God save the King.

With Ace Walker and Rick Forney of the Winnipeg Goldeyes.

Rick: "Thanks for the lesson. I feel confident tonight. I feel like I'm going to get it over the—what's it called again?"

Ace: "The plate . . ."

PENSION TENSION

January 24, 2012

Something fascinating happened this past week. The Canadian Taxpayers Federation attacked members of Parliament, saying their pensions were platinum plated. And then, among the political pundits, the people who are paid to disagree with one another, peace broke out. They all agreed: slash those pensions.

Now, I understand the sentiment. When I heard that Pierre Poilievre, Stephen Harper's favourite MP of all time, qualified for a full pension at thirty-one, I was physically ill. We have to ask ourselves, "Why did he qualify for a full pension at thirty-one?" Well, for starters, he got elected straight out of school. He had never accomplished anything of any note.

That's the type of person that's getting elected. People who have done nothing but are experts in everything. We avoid those people in real life, but for some reason the House of Commons is crawling with them.

So, let's just forget pensions. I want better MPs. I want the best and the brightest that Canada has to offer. And boy, is that not happening. And why? Well, the fact is, if you're mid-career with a family, leaving both behind and taking off to Ottawa for six or seven years is not good for either of them. There's a very good chance, at the end of the day, both will be seriously damaged. And are we going to fix this problem and attract better MPs by making the job less desirable? No. We go down that road and for every Pierre Poilievre, there'll be ten more just like him.

Now, don't get me wrong—I like beating up a lousy MP as much as the next guy. But when we get a good MP, they aren't just worth their pension, they're worth their weight in gold. All the parties have them, but they are few and far between. So, what say when it comes to MPs, instead of all of us piling on and lowering the bar, let's aim high for a change.

THE RACE TO DISENGAGEMENT

January 31, 2012

There's been a lot of talk over the last five years among political geeks about voter suppression. Convincing voters that politics is so nasty that, come election day, people just stay home. Now, up until now, to give them credit, nobody has ever accused the NDP of practising this dark art.

Well, that has certainly changed, because I don't think I have ever seen a greater example of voter suppression than the current NDP leadership race. It's like they designed it to disengage the public. Leadership races are tough on parties, but they're fun. They expose rifts. They lead to debate. Things are said in the heat of the moment that cause excitement, which makes people care. Not with this crowd.

As of last count, there were eight different candidates. And I use the term "different" very loosely. Because I don't know where you could find eight different Canadians who agree on as many things as these people. It's like the worst dinner party ever.

I watched the last leadership debate on streaming video. The most exciting moment happened at the forty-minute mark, when I got a pop-up ad for a

Liberty coin from the Franklin Mint. And the nastiest exchange so far came when front-runner Brian Topp, whom nobody knows, accused Thomas Mulcair of being—wait for it—a moderate. Whoa—those are fighting words. Can anyone on the left in this country make a fist?

I would like to say that there's a fine line between an exciting race and a race that is so dull it is actually detrimental to the democratic process, but there's not. There's a huge gaping divide. And unless the NDP can fix this and get people to pay attention, everyone loses. Because if you can't engage voters, you don't deserve voters.

ROOT'N TOOT'N ROB

February 14, 2012

The great thing about living in a modern democracy is that it is always changing. And I've got to hand it to the party in power: ever since we elected this strong, stable, majority government, we are getting brand new rights every single day.

Like this past week, the Minister of Justice, Rob Nicholson, stood up and announced, out of the blue, that if someone comes onto your property and you think they might be there to steal your all-terrain vehicle or catch your car on fire, you have the right to pick up a gun and fire warning shots at them.

Well, thank God that's cleared up. We all know what it's like: you look down the bottom of the driveway, you see someone funny. You don't know what they're up to. They could be a car burner. Now, I don't own an all-terrain vehicle, but I do own a barbecue, and I don't like to brag, but it's pretty nice. So next time someone comes into my yard—warning shot. And that goes for you, too, Mr. Knocking-on-My-Door-Looking-for-Twenty-Dollars-for-the-Cystic-Fibrosis-Walk-Just-When-I'm-Sitting-Down-to-Dinner. You could be a car burner—warning shot.

Now, the greatest threat to my life as a city dweller has nothing to do with people stealing my property, and everything to do with some idiot in a four-thousand-pound SUV who does not know how to use a signal light. Be warned: do that again, cut me off without signalling—warning shot. And while we're at it, people who do not walk in a straight line on the sidewalk, and people who get on an elevator before letting the people inside the elevator off the elevator—warning shots for the lot of you.

Yes, it's a brave new world. The Minister of Justice, Canada's top cop, is saying don't call the cops—fire at will. If you live across the street, you might want to duck.

Recreating 1812 at the Fanshawe Pioneer Village, London, Ontario.

Rick: "So, you have to bite [the tip] off every bullet?"

Private: "Yep."

Rick: "What if you had no teeth? Because *that* would be authentic."

Private: "To be a soldier, it was a requirement to have two teeth: one top, one bottom."

Rick: "That was a requirement? That's the same requirement I have on my eHarmony ad."

VIC LIKES TO WATCH

February 21, 2012

My guess is if the average citizen were told that they had five minutes left to live and they were alone in their house, a good percentage of Canadians would devote two or three of those last minutes on earth to erasing their hard drives. Not because they're criminals, but because it might contain something that's—what's the expression I'm looking for?—nobody's business.

And that includes the Minister of Public Safety, Vic Toews. Now Vic . . . Vic's a nice guy, but he's got this thing. He likes to peek. Or at least, he wants to peek into your hard drive. He wants to be able to get your computer's IP address without a warrant; he wants all of your computer online traffic recorded. It's his thing.

Vic says it's no big deal—it's like a phone book. Now, I trust Vic, I do, but I asked a computer geek friend of mine and he says no, it's nothing like a phone book. In fact, it's like a fingerprint. Except it's a fingerprint that can tell Vic how much money you make, what you read, where you get your news, what you say to your best friend, what turns you on and how you vote. Gee, is that all, Vic? Because, um, that makes me uncomfortable.

Now, Vic says we have a choice to make here. We can side with the Conservatives and let Vic peek, or we can side with the child pornographers. Unfortunately for Vic, he forgot one very important thing: Canadians aren't that stupid. And thank God. Because, Vic, you can call us all the names you want, but that doesn't change the fact we're not going to let you peek. That doesn't make us criminal; it makes us Canadian. It's why we shut our blinds at night.

The state has no business in the hard drives of the nation. You want to peek, Vic? Convince a judge and get a warrant.

THE BAR SINKS LOWER

February 28, 2012

I have always loved politics. Politics has always been my baseball. I love the competition. I love the ideas. I love the brilliance, the pomposity, and the idiocy of some of the great characters who practise the art. And I have always believed it's an art worth practising.

Now, I understand, in Canadian politics the bar is very low. Let's face it: you've got to get on your stomach and crawl to fit under there. But there has always been a little bit of sunshine. There's always been a little bit of light. This past week, I'm not so sure. I'm talking about robocalls.

We now know that, during the last federal election, hundreds of thousands of calls came out of Edmonton to Liberal and NDP voters in eighteen different ridings, claiming they were coming from Elections Canada, lying, sending people to voting booths that didn't exist. And what's really freaking me out is that I'm not angry. Which is a very bad sign, because anger is my cardio. I think I may be disappointed. Either that, or I'm having a stroke.

Now, I understand, in politics, there have always been dirty tricks. But this is not some drunks tearing down some posters. This is not even a negative ad campaign. This is big money and technology targeting people who want to vote and trying to physically stop them. We can't have this.

You put ten Canadians in a room, and they will disagree on ten things. Fine. But we have always agreed that voting is a fundamental right. This is not a left or right thing. This is just a thing. If we don't believe in that, what else do we have to believe in?

If stopping people who want to vote from doing so becomes the new normal, we will have hit a new low in the sewer that is Canadian politics. Keep this up, and we'll need a snorkel to get under that bar. Any deeper, and we all drown.

WHO'S THE GUILTY PARTY?

March 20, 2012

Like everyone else in Canada, I'm being worn down by this robocall scandal. It is as nasty as anything we have ever seen in Canadian politics. But like everyone else raised on episodes of *Law and Order*, I like my crimes discovered, investigated and solved within fifty-five minutes. No such luck.

Instead, week after week in the House of Commons, we're subjected to all the parties standing up and accusing all the other parties of destroying the democratic process. It's nauseating. When Dean Del Mastro opens his mouth, I want to punch myself in the face. I wouldn't be surprised if he stands up and blames my mother next.

But the truth is, for all the grandstanding, none of the MPs actually know what happened in the last election. They're MPs—the people who run the campaigns tell them nothing. You ask any MP, off the record, about what happened in the last election, and all you're told is, "I hope it wasn't us."

The problem is, the only people who can order a judicial inquiry are the cabinet. Which would mean investigating their own party. That's like asking Don

Cherry to donate his brain to science—it's not going to happen.

Luckily, we live in Canada and we have another option. It is a long shot, but it's a real shot: the Governor General. He is, by definition, above it all. Which is exactly what we need right now. With one stroke of the pen, he can say, "That's it, we're getting to the bottom of it—a Royal Commission." And why not? It's just our faith in democracy at stake, and let's face it, Stephen Harper loves everything with the word *royal* in it.

Because if we don't investigate this top to bottom, coast to coast, all the people out there that believe voting is useless will finally have their proof. And fans of voter suppression will have committed the perfect crime.

Snorkelling with salmon In the Campbell River, B.C.

Rick: "We're going to go swimming with the salmon. They're all up here spawning. They're checking each other out. They've been out in the ocean for an extended period of time and they're returning home to spawn. The opposite of what students are doing at this time of year."

PUBLIC SERVICE ANNOUNCEMENT

March 27, 2012

Consider this a public service announcement. If you found yourself this past week sitting at home on the couch, watching TV and relaxing, and suddenly you found yourself confronted by an attack ad paid for by the Conservative Party—do not panic. There is not a rift in the space-time continuum. You were not suffering a small stroke or cerebral hemorrhage. And no, there is no federal election imminent. You were simply experiencing the new normal in Canada: the never-ending campaign. Welcome to hell.

And I know we were all hoping that the constant barrage of negative advertising would end with the minority governments. No such luck. In the old days, prime ministers used to devote all of their time between elections to governing Canada. Not anymore. Now, a prime minister has negative ads to approve and reputations to destroy,. Being mean and cutthroat is not something you just do every four years. Now, it's a full-time job.

I admit, sometimes I don't understand political strategy. So I asked a Tory friend of mine: "Why? Why pay for attack ads three years before an election? And why attack Bob Rae, when the Liberals are in third place and he's got crazy scientist hair?" And the guy said, "Why not? We've got so much money, we could buy every ad available in a seven-game playoff series and the Olympics, and we'd still have more money left over than all the other parties combined." Great!

So I guess the moral of this story is that negative ads are never going away. Ever. If that's the case, may I make a suggestion? We used to refer to these things as "American-style" attack ads and "American-style" dirty tricks. I think it's time we gave our friends to the south a break. It is the new reality: attack ads and dirty tricks aren't just American anymore. They're Canadian as Canadian can be.

The Winners of the sixth annual ***Spread*** the Net Student Challenge were: *Lakefield Elementary School, Quispamsis, New Brunswick, with $15,884.47; Peterborough Colligate and Vocational School, Peterborough, Ontario, with $52,661.60; and McGill University, Montreal, Quebec, with $9,147.52.* ***Spread the Net*** *aims to educate Canadians about malaria and raise funds to buy bed nets. For more details and news of future Challenges, go to spreadthenet.org.*

WE NEED MORE SCHOOLS LIKE THIS

April 3, 2012

It's been a very long time since I've been in school. And like a lot of Canadians, when I see a yellow bus, I breathe into a paper bag and then I carry on with my day. But this past week, I went back to school. And why not? Forty-seven schools from across Canada came together and raised a quarter of a million dollars for kids on the other side of the planet. And I know, it was a contest—"Who can raise the most money?" But let's face it: no matter where you go to school, there's always going to be a school that's bigger, nicer, richer, whatever. The kids know this, and yet they still went to work and raised all that money.

Really, what is wrong with kids today? From where I'm standing, not much. And how about the kids at Peterborough Collegiate and Vocational School? What a school! Great sports, great science, they got arts up the yazoo. They have an anti-bullying hotline that hasn't been called in eleven months. And still, this year, they were told out of the blue that their school was closing.

You know, in these situations, you have two options. You can do what you're told or you can fight like hell. These kids, they went with the latter, and boy, what a beautiful sight. They fought, they marched, they made the lives of the school board a living hell, and they still went out and raised fifty grand for kids in Africa.

These kids may not be able to vote, but they could teach us all a thing or two about being engaged citizens. In fact, if I could replace the entire federal cabinet with thirty-nine kids from PCVS, I would do it in a heartbeat.

I take that back. I would replace them with *twenty-five* kids. Harper's cabinet is too big as it is.

The president of the student council at PCVS has said they're going to keep fighting because Canada needs more schools like theirs, not one fewer. I tend to agree. I'm just glad they lasted as long as they did. We're all better off because of it.

Acknowledgements: The Book

Thanks to publisher Kristin Cochrane, publicist Cathy Paine, designer C.S. Richardson, and the rest of the Doubleday Canada team for continuing to make authorship such a pleasure. My editor at Doubleday was again Tim Rostron, a godlike genius in his handling of everything from the big picture to such details as the drafting of this sentence.

Above and beyond the considerable demands of their day jobs, publisher's assistant Kiara Kent at Doubleday, RMR script co-ordinator Kevin Drysdale and CBC publicist David McCaughna were invaluable in directing the traffic of words and pictures.

Acknowledgements: The Show

Five years ago I wrote the acknowledgements to my first *RMR* book and I am struck with how similar the list is this time around.

The reason is very simple. I have always believed the most important secret to success in show business is to surround yourself with the very best in the business and then try like hell to keep them on board. I'm proud to say that since that last book I've managed to do that with pretty much everyone, the glaring exception being the very talented comedy writer Irwin Barker who left the show in 2011. It wasn't personal; he passed away after a stunningly impressive battle with cancer. We miss him very much.

Gerald Lunz is still the executive producer and my partner in crime. He is still the funniest man in the room and still the man who edits and fixes every rant I write. Why he hasn't gotten tired of that or me I shall never know, but I am eternally grateful.

Chris Finn, Tim Steeves, Greg Eckler, Rick Currie and George Westerhom are the lads in the writers' room. Imagine getting to hang out with the funniest people you know week in and week out, that's my job. Good gig.

Our supervising producer Tom Stanley continues to be

a mission-critical part of the team. If he goes, I go. I say this despite the fact that it was his idea that I get tasered for the show—a segment that never aired. I cannot tell you the contributions he has made to our success since coming on board.

Under Tom's thumb and direction are Nik Sexton and Scott Stephenson, the youngest, smartest and best-dressed part of the office.

I still head out on the road every week with the same brilliant crew, cameraman Don Spence and road director John Marshall. Michal Grajewski came on board a few years back because we are old and tend to fall asleep at the wheel, and he is young and can go days without sleep. He is also the show's photographer, camera assistant and improv director. He talks about the Winnipeg Jets just a little too much.

Al Maclean and Miles Davren take the tape we shoot at *RMR* and edit it in a way that makes me look way better than I deserve to.

The CBC graphics department of Mike Burroughs, Jake Boone and Jodi Boyer astound me every week, both with the quality of their work and the tight schedule they are required to do it in.

The production team of Alan MacGillivary and Marilyn Richardson continue to make the office and the show appear to run like clockwork, mostly because they tell Gerald and me nothing. I thank you for that.

Henry Sarwer-Foner continues after twenty years to be my director and is the reason why everything shot in the *RMR* studio looks so great.

And then there are the people at *RMR* who make their own jobs look easy when they are anything but: Baron Evans, Nan Brown, Kelli McNeil, Bob Graham, Brian Barlow, Kye Fox, Meliase Patterson, Jill Aslin, Terry Hanlon, Jon Sturge, Claire Wing and—thanks again—Kevin Drysdale and David McCaughna.

At the CBC I continue to be indebted to Kirsten Stewart and George Anthony. Kirsten for being such a supporter and George for knowing more about show business than anyone I know. And as always, we are so lucky to be able to work with one of the great TV production crews, the men and women at the CBC Broadcast Centre in Toronto.

And to all the great actors whom have come into our studio and played with me over the years, there are too many of you to mention, but it is always a privilege to share the boards with you.

And to those friends who I tend to bother on a Thursday night when I am supposed to be writing a rant but instead I am staring at a blank screen, thank you for picking up when you know it's me calling—especially John Ratchford and Shirley Douglas.

And for anyone who has watched a rant and said "Right on—good job" or "That guy should be fired"—I thank you too for watching and listening.